SERMONS

from Thanksgiving to Easter

SERMONS

from Thanksgiving to Easter

DAVID A. MacLENNAN

THE JUDSON PRESS

Valley Forge

SERMONS FROM THANKSGIVING TO EASTER

To my fellow-Christians
who witness in pulpit
and pew to the Gospel
of Christ,
I dedicate these sermons
with admiration and love.

CONTENTS

Enlighten our minds with thy truth, and cap-
ture our hearts with thy love; through Jesus
Christ our Lord. Amen.

TAKEN INVENTORY LATELY?

SCRIPTURE: "How precious to me are thy thoughts, O God! How vast is the sum of them! If I would count them, they are more than the sand, When I awake, I am still with thee" (Psalm 139:17-18).

"Praise be to God for giving us through Christ every possible spiritual benefit as citizens of Heaven! For consider what he has done — before the foundation of the world he chose us to become, in Christ, his holy and blameless children living within his constant care. . . . And here is the staggering thing — that in all which will one day belong to him we have been promised a share" (Ephesians 1:3-5, 11, Phillips).

"Have you taken inventory lately?" The question was asked in an old-fashioned grocery store where I worked. Supermarkets, shopping plazas, and vast chain stores were still in the future, at least in that community. At thirteen I had my first paying job. Job description? Every Saturday to be a handy boy around the place. This particular morning I was sweeping the floor when I heard the senior partner, the father of the junior partner, ask about the business. What caught my attention was a question: "Taken inventory lately?" The answer was, "Yes, sir." When the opportune moment arrived, I asked the kindly older man, "What is an inventory?" Patiently he explained: "It's making a list of all you have in the store — all the groceries on the shelves and in the basement, wrapping paper, string, everything. An inventory is counting up all you've got."

"Taken inventory lately?" It is a good question to ask when we brood overmuch on all we have not acquired by way of assets. It is a salutary exercise when we are tempted to whine or repine, or indulge in self-pity. In one of the most beautiful of all poems, the 139th Psalm, the author celebrates the everywhereness of God. He marvels at God's complete knowledge and care of his creatures. God the Creator, God whose loving presence is in the heights and in the depths, also shaped us in our prenatal state. The statement in the 139th Psalm may not be scientifically precise, but this Psalm is not intended to be a scientific treatise. The author is saying, "While I was but an embryonic speck, he took charge of me and knitted together my bodily frame." [1]

Then the sheer wonder of God's knowledge and love sparks a shout of praise:

"How precious to me are thy thoughts, O God!
How vast is the sum of them!
If I would count them, they are more than the sand."
(Psalm 139:17-18)

Have you taken inventory lately? Today is Thanksgiving Sunday. From time to time, and not just on our annual celebration, we should at least start to take inventory. Remember the old hymn:

"Count your many blessings, name them one by one,
And it will surprise you what the Lord hath done."

In the New Testament letter to the young church in Ephesus, the apostle writes, as J. B. Phillips superbly translates his Greek: "Praise be to the God and Father of our Lord Jesus Christ for giving us through Christ every possible spiritual benefit as citizens of Heaven! For consider what he has done — before the foundation of the world he chose us to become, in Christ, his holy and blameless children living within his constant care. . . . And here is the staggering thing — that in all which will one day belong to him we have been promised a share" (Ephesians 1:3-4, 11).

Let's begin our inventory. Admittedly we will run out of time before we run out of every possible benefit.

Let us begin with life itself. In the prayer of General Thanksgiving we "give . . . most humble and hearty thanks for all thy goodness and loving-kindness to us, and to all men. We bless thee for our creation. . . ." Without asking "by your leave" God started this whole amazing and still mysterious process of our creation. He gave us a high place on the scale of living creatures. He endowed us with minds to think, hearts to love, spirits to

[1] Frank H. Ballard in *The Interpreter's Bible* (New York: Abingdon Press, 1955), Vol. 4, p. 716.

10

aspire. He gave us what we call conscience, so that we could not live comfortably by the law of the jungle, although we sometimes revert to it. We can look backward, forward, and upward. We are made in his spiritual likeness; we are more than animals. No one ever pats a crocodile on the back and urges it to do its best by saying, "Be a crocodile, old fellow." There is no likelihood that it will be anything else. But we do rally a young fellow by putting a friendly hand on his shoulder and saying, "Be a man, son." Beauty, truth, goodness, and courage are meaningful to us. God gave us memory so that we might have roses in December. Thank God for life!

"For our creation, preservation . . ." We do have something to do with our preservation. So have countless others: our parents, other members of the family, our teachers, research scientists, physicians, surgeons, nurses, hospital staff, government representatives, the police, and the military forces. Moreover, God has given us intelligence, so that we cross on the green light and still watch traffic. We obey the rules of health. Sometimes we have been hurt, injured, made sick. Sometimes we have come close to abject failure of one kind or another: financial failure, marital failure, moral failure, mental failure. But deliverance came. We were rescued, delivered, preserved. This is why we thank God for our preservation, acknowledging gratefully that God uses human agents and instruments. This truth is expressed clearly in the following words: "When you say to me 'Thank you,' remember I could not have done for you what I did if it had not been for what hundreds of other people have done for me. Neither could they have done for me what they did had it not been for what thousands of other people had done for them. And so the thing goes on in infinite time and space. Therefore, when you say 'Thank you,' you really mean to say 'Thank you, God.'"

"And all the blessings of this life." If you were to take inventory of them all, you would find yourself echoing the psalmist: "How vast is the sum of them! If I would count them, they are more than the sand" (Psalm 139:17-18). So much we take for granted. A physician once told me that at a convention of some five thousand specialists in New York City the doctors were informed that medical research in drugs and medicines has advanced so rapidly in a short time that one half of all prescriptions

written that year could not have been written five years ago! All the blessings of this life are ours — food, clothing, housing, music, drama, the arts, work to do, more adequate provision for more people all the time — notwithstanding vast areas of need around the earth. What of our country's heritage? We have responsible and representative government, trial by jury, and ordered freedom. What of the blessing of friendship? Of love of men and women?

When you take inventory of the blessings of this life, *be sure to count in the things which did not come to you!* Remember the thing, the situation you feared? The sickness? The result of tests in the hospital? The rumored transfer to another department or city? And the clouds that were filled with dread proved to be full of opportunity or mercy.

The General Thanksgiving moves into the depth of God's love and up to the heights of gratitude: "But above all, for thine inestimable love in the redemption of the world by our Lord Jesus Christ; for the means of grace, and for the hope of glory." "Do we need salvation?" a thoughtful man asked me not long ago. Do we? Well, do we need health? Do we need deliverance from a sense of guilt? Do we need to be saved into a life harmonious, unified, free, and moving toward some worthy goal? Recall the popular novel by Sloan Wilson, *The Man in the Gray Flannel Suit.* Tom Rath, the hero, is applying for a new job. He feels that he is getting along famously with the oral interview until the personnel man, Walker, throws him a curve. Walker says he wants Tom to do him the little favor of writing his autobiography. Even that seems possible, because Tom is informed that he will have an hour for the assignment. He relaxes a bit, until Walker puts the finishing touch on the assignment by concluding that Tom can write anything in this autobiography, but at the end of the last page he is to finish this sentence: "*The most significant fact about me is. . . .*" That part of the assignment proves almost devastating to Tom Rath. How would you do it? "The most significant fact about me is. . . ."

In the Bible you will find ancient equivalents of personnel men trying to help us to give the correct ending to the sentence. "Thou hast made him [man] little less than God, and dost crown him with glory and honor" (Psalm 8:5). The most significant fact about me is that the Lord of all my life has shown me that the highest good is "to do justice, and to love kindness, and to walk humbly with your God" (Micah 6:8). The most significant fact about me is that now am I a son of God and it does not yet appear what I might become. . . . Ask the great apostle, and you will hear him say "The Son of God . . . loved me and gave himself for me" (Galatians 2:20). *The most significant fact about me is that I am loved — loved so much.* The arms of the cross stretch out into infinity as if to say that this love, with which you have been loved, is endless, unfailing. Ask Paul, and he answers in the words of our New Testament text: "Praise be to the God and Father of our Lord Jesus Christ for giving us through Christ every possible spiritual benefit as citizens of Heaven!" "For consider what he has done — before the foundation of the world he chose us to become, in Christ, his holy and blameless children [I have my doubts about that holy and blameless bit until I remember his forgiveness and his grace] living within his constant care. . . ." Said Christ, "You did not choose me, but I chose you," to be my men and women, to live useful fruitful lives (cf. John 15:16). The most significant fact about you and me is that we are loved by God, loved so much that Christ died for us. Paul takes it up; you would think he was really in the jet stream, gaining altitude every second: "And here is the staggering thing — that in all which will one day belong to him we have been promised a share." So consider what God has done, and be thankful.

"For the means of grace, and the hope of glory." Aren't you counting them too? Prayer, the Bible and Bible study, worship, the service we can render as members of this church as we take our place in the community on Monday through Saturday? George Bernard Shaw once characterized some church congregations as groups of hermits coming into the sanctuary, each person bringing his own cup of self-satisfaction to be filled, and then carrying the filled cup back to his cave to be devoured. That is a caricature. It is not vital Christianity. Our Lord sought renewal in both private prayer and social worship; often he drew back from the crowd that he might have his cup filled to overflowing. He took it back not to supply his own needs but that he might share the life-renewing wine of God's power and love with others.

Have you taken inventory lately? Consider what God has done.

PRAYER: O God, who gives us life, give us also hearts filled with thankfulness. We pray in the grace of Jesus Christ our Lord. Amen.

Come to us, O Lord, in words spoken and received, and in the bread and wine of the sacrament of thy love. Amen.

WHERE TO GO AT CHRISTMAS?
TO A TABLE

SCRIPTURE: "You are those who have continued with me in my trials; as my Father appointed a kingdom for me, so do I appoint for you that you may eat and drink at my table in my kingdom, and sit on thrones judging [ruling] the twelve tribes of Israel" (Luke 22:28-30).

Boys and girls in kindergarten and primary department classes of church school were asked what they liked most about Christmas. Their answers included both what you and I would expect and what we would not expect! One young lady said, "I like it when we have company." Another small girl answered, "I like helping to get the dinner ready."

Where best to go at Christmas? To a table, where we can eat together with our family and perhaps with others, too.

On this first Sunday in the season of Advent, on the first of the four Sundays preceding Christmas Day, we endorse the little girl's preference. One place to which we enjoy going is a table, with food and friends and family gathered to celebrate and recall other good times together.

In the heart of Christian worship and at the heart of Christian life is a table — the table of the Lord. What we do in this sacrament began at a table in an upper room reached by an outside stair in a Jerusalem home. It was Passover time in the capital city. Jesus had arranged for the use of the room so that he could have one last meal with his students. He used ancient symbols in the last meal together. He gave to the ancient symbols a new meaning. He took bread, and said "This is my body." *This is what we mean by a sacrament.* A sacrament is some *thing*, usually a familiar thing. Perhaps it is a very ordinary thing which has new meaning for a person of insight and understanding. Have you at home a drawer, or a box, or a trunk, or a chest containing a lot of old things? Perhaps the man of the house calls the contents "junk," although men are often as reluctant as women to part with old keepsakes, souvenirs, mementos. Some of these have almost sacramental meaning. In November, 1963, a hushed nation and world watched through television the last rites for our late President John F. Kennedy. During the committal service in Arlington Cemetery, the honor guard reverently folded the flag which had draped the coffin of President Kennedy and gave it to Mrs. Kennedy. Flags are familiar, even commonplace. But this particular flag was invested with new significance. All her life, that section of red, white, and blue cloth would speak to Mrs. Kennedy of the man she loved. It would speak to the children of the father they loved. Isn't this what makes something a sacrament? The bread we take at the sacrament is common bread, but for a person with understanding and feeling the bread signifies the very body of Christ; it speaks of his life laid down; it speaks of the body Jesus created through his life, his teaching, his sacrificial death, and his resurrection.

On the table also was a *cup*. He took the cup, saying, "This cup is the new covenant made at the price of my blood." In the Bible, as you know, a covenant is a relationship between God and man. Man entered into an agreement with God; he made certain vows or pledges. God entered into an agreement with man. But man could not keep his part of the agreement. His sin, his failures in love, broke the relationship. In Old Testament days a whole sacrificial system was devised to restore the shattered bond. Sacrifice, it was hoped, would restore the broken relationship. Then Jesus said: My life, my death, make possible the restoration of the broken relationship. You are sinners, but I have died for you. God is no longer your enemy; but your friend. You will forget this, because you are human. Time tends to erase even vivid experiences. Come into my house sometimes. In its peaceful stillness, and with the visible reminders of what I have used and said and done, you will remember me. You will realize that I am with you always.

At that last meal together there was a traitor. At that table there was bickering and strife among those for whom Jesus was willing to die. Imagine a family gathered together for Christmas dinner and all during the meal the adult members arguing as to which was the greatest, best loved, and most important member of the circle! How tragic it was that in the very shadow of the death of the head of the family, and in his presence, such quarreling should take place! A seminary professor observed that there is more argument about precedence, and more concern about people's places, in the church than anywhere else. But the first church members learned a lesson they could not ever quite forget. It is a lesson we need constantly to review.

Where to go at Christmas? To a table; to the Lord's Table. Why is this Table, as children are wont to say, so special?

First, because of the Host. Jesus is the Host. It is the Lord's Table, not this church's, nor the table of our particular denomination. It is *his* Table. Whosoever will may come, who comes not to express his opinions but to seek a Presence; not because he feels good and saintly, but because he knows he is a sinner and needs a Savior and forgiveness. With reverence, thanksgiving, joy, and love we come to a living Lord and Friend. This is not merely commemoration of Jesus Christ; it is *communion* with him.

We come to the Table to learn and relearn that *God, who gave us Jesus Christ, is Love.* It is said that love is something you do; and God has done the most to bring us newness of life, to assure us that we are loved creatures. Thus this simple, beautiful, symbolic meal is an enactment of the gospel. It is the Word made visible.

We come to the Table in Advent and Christmas as at every other time *because this Table is surrounded by the most interesting, most wonderful kind of guests.* Here, although we cannot see them all, are men and women and boys and girls of every color and language, of every degree of culture, of every level of Christian growth, of every profession and trade and vocation. Here our economic, social, political, racial, educational differences — even our religious differences — are forgotten and transcended. Certainly they should be forgotten. Assuredly the Spirit of God transcends every distinction. We are one in Christ. We are the family and household of God. We are in the communion of all the faithful in heaven and on earth.

We come to this table *to realize that Jesus was right: It is not the king, not the top leader, but the servant who obtains the highest title in Christ's kingdom.* Only the person who is willing to serve will rise to the heights. Does anyone ever really love the man who is out for himself all the time? Do you really love the person who is forever getting or trying to get, but who is rarely giving?

So we come to the Lord's Table as the Christmas season begins: *to offer sacrifices* of praise and thanksgiving along with the bread and wine.

And we make the most meaningful offering of all, as the Lord gives us his grace. What is this? It is ourselves. In every order for the Lord's Supper, whether it is called the Mass, the Divine Liturgy, Holy Communion, or the Eucharist, the heart of the service is the point at which the presiding servant says, "And here we offer and present unto thee, O Lord, our selves, our souls and bodies, to be a reasonable, holy, and living sacrifice. . . ." It is *reasonable.* After all, God in Christ gave himself. We now give ourselves through Christ. The gift is *holy.* It links the divine with the human. It is *living.* It is our very selves.

We come to the Table of the Lord to gain strength for the next stage of our journey. We feed on him in our hearts by faith. By his grace divine we all are fed.

Where to go at Christmas? *To a Table.* To the table of the Lord as we do today. We are guests of God, the God who meets us in the Lord Jesus Christ. Go to his table because our divine Host is Love and loving. Go to the table where we sit beside those of every group and class and race and nation who have responded to his call: the people of God. We go not because we are good or important, but because we have gladly enrolled among God's people as servants of God and our neighbors. We go because we can offer the gift that God considers the most precious gift of all, the one gift he can use — ourselves.

"You are those who have continued with me in my trials;" says our Lord, "as my Father appointed a kingdom for me, so do I appoint for you that you may eat and drink at my table in my kingdom . . ." (Luke 22:28-30).

PRAYER: O God, whose dear Son Jesus Christ made himself known to his disciples in the breaking of bread, we give thee thanks that thou hast opened the eyes of our faith that we may recognize thee at this table and in every place and in all thy children; in Jesus Christ our Lord. Amen.

Help us now to listen to Thy Word, O God, to understand and to obey: through Christ our Lord. Amen.

WHERE TO GO AT CHRISTMAS?
TO A BOOKSTORE

SCRIPTURE: "Please bring with you . . . the books, especially the manuscripts" (2 Timothy 4:13, Phillips).

"Please bring the books," wrote the apostle Paul to his friend and younger colleague Timothy. Whoever may have been the actual writer of the two letters to Timothy, the mind and concern are those of the apostle Paul. Into these letters are woven notes of actual correspondence Paul had with Timothy. This relationship is particularly apparent in the fourth chapter of the second letter to Timothy. Listen then to Paul, speaking of his approaching end. He has reached the finish line and looks forward to the prize, the crown of life eternal. He gives Timothy various personal messages. "And please bring with you the cloak I left with Carpus at Troas, and the books, especially the manuscripts."

We would like to know what the books were. Considerable speculation has been provoked by the reference. He wanted the books. The word actually used is *biblia,* which literally means "papyrus rolls." Could it be that these rolls contained the earliest forms of the Gospels? Paul also wanted the *parchments.* These might have been legal documents which Paul needed in prison, such as his certificate of Roman citizenship. Scholars are inclined to think it more likely that they were copies of the Hebrew Scriptures, the Old Testament. It is known that the Hebrews wrote their sacred books on rolls of parchment made from the skins of animals. When Paul was in prison waiting for death, he wanted most of all the word of God.

What do you imagine you would want if, like St. Paul and many another, you were nearing the end of the road, needing desperately something to put strength and courage into your soul? You may find an answer by facing another question:

Where to go at Christmas? I suggest: *to a bookstore.* Why not to a library? Libraries are indispensable, but libraries do not give you books for keeps. Some books should be bought, for others and for ourselves. Why to a bookstore? Because, like the apostle, we need the knowledge and the power which good books offer. This is a not-too-subtle way of urging you to *buy a Bible, and use it.*

You say: "But I have a Bible, even if I don't read it as I should." Isn't it possible that one of the reasons you may not read the Bible is that you need to buy a new copy, a copy of a new translation of the Scriptures? Time was when every church-related family owned a family Bible. Often it was as large as an unabridged dictionary. It was a symbol of the family tradition and it contained special pages that provided a kind of family tree. Vital statistics were written in it: births, marriages, deaths. (In our new Bibles we would do well to keep such family records.) Sometimes it was also a repository for pressed leaves and other keepsakes. In an earlier era such a Bible was used in family worship. But times have changed, and so have Bibles. I can hear some discerning lover of pure and undefiled English protest: You can't seriously contend that any of the new versions are in the same league with the King James Version as far as English is concerned? No, I agree that for elegance of diction and majestic English as spoken in the age of the first Queen Elizabeth and of Shakespeare, the King James Version stands in a class of its own. But as a Bible teacher has pointed out, when we have even a beautifully bound copy of the King James Version, we reverently tend to enshrine it on a shelf as though we expected its presence there to bless us by some sort of spiritual emanation. Can we expect to be nourished by food in a can if we never open the can? If the Bible is to be a source of spiritual strength it must (in the words of the famous Anglican prayer) be read, marked, learned, and inwardly digested.

One of the hindrances to taking the Bible out of its container — at least for many of us — is the obscure language of the King James Version. Nearly two hundred years ago Benjamin Franklin noted this. He said that one reason Bible reading had come to be neglected was that the language and style of the King James Version were obsolete. It isn't enough to be sentimentally attached to a noble monument of English prose. Moreover, new translations are necessary because we now possess manuscripts of the New Testament which are a thousand years older than anything from which the King James Version was made; these manuscripts are a thousand years nearer the originals, and therefore much more accurate.

Examine some of the more recent translations in a bookstore, or a church library. The Revised Standard Version stands as close to the King James as it is possible to stand and still be natural, clear, and smooth in style. It has dignity and simplicity, and certainly is suited for private study and for use in public worship. There are also several other fresh translations: the entire Bible as translated by the famous scholar James Moffatt; the New Testament translated by Richard Weymouth, the translation by Helen Barrett Montgomery, *The New English Bible*, the Phillips translation, the American Bible Society's translation of the New Testament, officially called *Today's English Version* and popularly named *Good News for Modern Man*, and others.

If you have only the King James Version, I earnestly urge you to buy another translation. Usually the newer versions are printed in more attractive format and more readable type. Moreover, such works as *The New English Bible* (at present only the New Testament is available) are not revisions of the older translations but are new translations. Like the Revised Standard Version, *The New English Bible* is the work of many scholars of great learning. It is a great achievement. *The New Testament in Modern English* by J. B. Phillips is done by one man, who used the language of the man in the street rather than the scholar in his study or the man in a pew. This language is frequently vivid, sometimes powerful, and more than once sharp in insight. True, Phillips does resort to paraphrase, but any good scholar must do this at times. Its down-to-earthness makes it less suited to liturgical use in public worship, but in personal reading and study it can shake us up. Best of all, the various translations are now available in inexpensive paperback editions.

Where to go at Christmas? To a bookstore to buy a copy of the Bible in a new translation. With it you might well place a copy of one of the very helpful commentaries on the Bible, or an introduction to the Bible. One of the highly recommended introductions and brief commentaries is the *Oxford Annotated Bible*. It is based on the Revised Standard Version, which it contains, and it has short introductions to each book, with many helpful footnotes. Valuable extra material is added, including an article, "How to Read the Bible." Other books to interpret the Bible are available. Your minister or a theological professor will gladly recommend some.

It may help you to choose a Bible if you consider a few passages from the versions mentioned:

John 1:1. King James Version: "In the beginning was the Word, and the Word was with God, and the Word was God." Revised Standard Version: "In the beginning was the Word, and the Word was with God, and the Word was God." *The New English Bible:* "When all things began, the Word already was. The Word dwelt with God, and what God was, the Word was." Phillips Translation: "At the beginning God expressed himself. That personal expression, that word, was with God and was God. . . ."

James 3:1. King James Version: "My brethren, be not many masters, knowing that we shall receive the greater condemnation." Revised Standard Version: "Let not many of you become teachers, my brethren, for you know that we who teach shall be judged with greater strictness." *The New English Bible:* "My brothers, not many of you should become teachers, for you may be certain that we who teach shall ourselves be judged with greater strictness." Phillips Translation: "Don't aim at adding to the number of teachers, my brothers, I beg you! Remember that we who are teachers will be judged by a much higher standard."

2 Corinthians 12:13. King James Version: "For what is it wherein ye were inferior to other churches, except it be that I myself was not burdensome to you? forgive me this wrong." Revised Standard Version: "For in what were you less favored than the rest of the churches, except that I myself did not burden you? Forgive me this wrong!" *The New English Bible:* "Is there anything in which you were treated worse than the other congregations — except this, that I never sponged upon you? How unfair of me! I crave forgiveness." Phillips Translation: "What makes you feel so inferior to other churches? Is it because I have not allowed you to support me financially? My humblest apologies for this great wrong!"

Let me now ask: *Why buy a Bible in a recent translation at Christmas — or at any time — for yourself, for a member of the family, or for a friend?* It is not just because we venerate this little library of sixty-six books. The Christian answer is, bluntly: *You and I need to own a Bible and to read it regularly, intelligently, imaginatively, and expectantly, because the words of the Bible contain the Word of God.* But aren't the words of the Bible undeniably human words? Yes. Each section bears the stamp of the author's personality. Much in the biblical writings is human and time-bound. Then, how can human words contain the Word of God?

When the man we know as St. Augustine was young and, as we say, "on the town" most of the time, he studied the Scriptures for a clue to life's meaning. From the Bible he turned eagerly to studies of current philosophies. Why? Because he said they, the Scriptures, appeared unworthy to be compared with the dignity of Cicero. But later, in a crisis of doubt and despair, he went back to the Bible and read Romans 13:13-14, and for the first time heard the words as if they were spoken to him. They were a command addressed to him personally: "Put on the Lord Jesus Christ." The Word stepped from the pages, recreated his life. Through a word of the Bible he heard the Word of God. The Word of God is always personal and specific. Come down to the twentieth century, to World War II, and see how the Bible speaks to our particular condition, often in a most amazing way. Bishop Berggrav told of his arrest by the Nazis during their occupation of his country, Norway. He was sitting in his house with a friend when there came the dreaded knock at the door. He went and opened the door, and there was a German officer with a guard and a waiting car. The Bishop put on his overcoat, went down the steps, and got in. As the car drew off, his friend called out: "Remember 1 Peter 3:13 and 14." Sitting beside the Nazi officer, Bishop Berggrav took out his New Testament and read: "Now who is there to harm you if you are zealous for what is right? But even if you do suffer for righteousness' sake, you will be blessed. Have no fear of them, nor be troubled, but in your hearts reverence Christ as Lord." It was a Word of God. Quietly he reverenced Christ as Lord in his heart and was at peace. In every case the Word meets the needs of people. In biblical thought the Word of God can be said to be nothing less than the life and power of God directed with a creative purpose into a specific human situation. John tells us that the creative Word took human form and became incarnate — embodied — in

Jesus Christ. "The Word became flesh and dwelt among us . . . we have beheld his glory" (John 1:14).

The Word of God is God in action. The Scriptures are the record of this primary divine activity. When you read the Bible in the light of this concept of the Word, it takes on new reality. It ceases to be a handbook on morals or a kind of holy Bartlett's *Familiar Quotations.* It becomes rather more like a continuous witness to the creative presence of God in human lives and history which spans twenty centuries. It is more than a record of what and how God spoke to men and within men long ago; It brings us into contact with the power of God in personal living. It is a means of grace, a channel by which God reaches men. Words of the Bible are changed into acts of God. To receive the full impact of the living Word, we must have both the Old Testament and the New. The law, the prophets, and the writings of the Old Testament promised the Messiah. When Jesus Christ, who was the Word made flesh, came, he was the fulfillment of God's promise which Israel had been expecting for centuries. The struggle of the Old Testament is completed with the victorious Christ of the New Testament.

You and I need to go to a bookstore and buy a copy of the Bible. We then need to *read it with faith.* The Bible itself points out that we proceed from faith to faith. When we read it with faith we can see ourselves in the sins, the struggles, and the victories of ancient Israel. It then becomes not only ancient history but *our* personal history.

Are we to go to a bookstore at Christmas to buy only a Bible, or even more than one Bible? No. A good book is not only the precious lifeblood of a master spirit; it may be a mind stretcher, a liberator of the mind and spirit. When you have serious doubts about the validity of the faith, you may be helped by counseling with a Christian through his book or by reading an exposition of the Christian faith. The late Professor Halford Luccock, my friend and former colleague, once meditated on that old standby among Christmas songs, "The Twelve Days of Christmas." He was sure that there was a profound philosophy of giving in the lines:

> "On the first day of Christmas my true love gave to me
> A partridge in a pear tree."

Dr. Luccock said that it celebrated "the high wisdom of completely inappropriate and largely useless gifts. . . . A partridge in a pear tree — what on earth could one do with that? . . . So take a suggestion for your own shopping list. Give your true love an inappropriate gift. Don't get grandma another lace cap or pair of woolen mittens. . . . She hates the things. Get her a set of lipsticks or a pair of dancing slippers. That will boost her morale. . . . As you reach for that fine book for your beloved pastor, the learned tome, *Archaeology and the Bible*, stay your hand. Reach over to the next counter and get him . . . a book of cartoons. . . . There are few joys greater than that of stepping out of character for a time. . . . The best gifts of love are those which show a lovely lack of common sense." [1] What wife and mother hasn't muttered something about a gift being impractical and loved it all the more because it was!

Halford Luccock knew that there was a high precedent for this: "The first Christmas gift was highly inappropriate — a Baby in a barn. Who wanted that? No one clapped his hands and said, 'Goody, goody, just what I wanted!' That is, no one except a few souls who could really see — Simeon and Anna in the Temple, some shepherds, his mother." [2]

But the hopes and fears of all the years are bound up in God's unsurpassable gift of himself in Jesus Christ.

PRAYER: O God of Infinite Surprises, we thank thee for the Bible, and for thy living Word, thy life, thy presence, which finds us and changes us and sustains us through the Scriptures of the faith, even the Word of God which became a human being in Jesus Christ. Help us to read thy book listening for a voice, *thy* voice. Amen.

[1] Halford E. Luccock, *Like A Mighty Army: Selected Letters of Simeon Stylites* (New York: Oxford University Press, 1954), pp. 16-18. Copyright 1951 Christian Century Foundation. Used by permission.
[2] *Ibid.*

*Capture our minds with thy truth and kindle
our hearts with thy love, that we may know
thee better and love thee more, in Jesus Christ
our Lord. Amen.*

WHERE TO GO AT CHRISTMAS?
TO A HOUSE

SCRIPTURE: "And the ransomed of the Lord shall return,
and come to Zion with singing,
with everlasting joy upon their heads;
they shall obtain joy and gladness,
and sorrow and sighing shall flee away" (Isaiah 35:10).

"The redeemed shall . . . come home to Zion singing, crowned
with an unending joy . . ." (Isaiah 35:9, 10, Moffatt).

In the thirty-fifth chapter of the Book of Isaiah, the writer
exults in God's final intervention in the tangled history of his
people. Because God's judgment is accompanied by deliverance,
the response of the prophet is a lyric of confidence and joy. At
the heart of ancient Israel's dream of a Messiah and his kingdom
has been the picture of going home. Deeper than any desire for
vengeance on their enemies and greater than the excitement of
victory has been the comfort of God's promise that they would
return to their homeland, their home!

It is a dream that human beings know. We often feel homeless
under the sun and lay our heads in a foreign land when day is
done. Ask of John Q. and Jane Citizen where they want to go
at Christmas? Wouldn't nine out of ten say quickly: Why, home,
of course! To a house where they'll be welcomed no matter what
they have done or failed to do. It's not only true of the ransomed
of the Lord, those whom the Bible calls the redeemed. When
I was only a year or so out of seminary and in my first parish
in a suburb of Boston, a promoter invited me to engage in debate
in the Boston Opera House with Bertrand Russell, the English
philosopher, mathematician, and earl. Being brash, I accepted.
One conversation I had with Lord Russell has remained in my

memory. Following a review of the rules of debate which we were to observe, he mentioned that he must leave for England on the same night. I asked if any emergency made it necessary for him to return so quickly. He looked at me in surprise and then explained: "A man wants to be home for Christmas." A man who was an agnostic, who rejected the Christian faith and interpretation of life, wanted to go to a house in England at Christmas — to his home.

Where to go at Christmas? To a house that is a home.

The first house is a strange one. It is no house at all, not even a lodging house or hotel. *It is a stable,* perhaps in a cave, as was frequently the case in Eastern lands. Piety and imagination have inspired art to give us idealized pictures of what it might have been like. Chances are, if Joseph and Mary reached Bethlehem in the bleak midwinter as the carol assumes, you could see steam rising from the straw from the animals stabled there. You would endure the distinctive smells you find in barns. And in one stall Joseph, perhaps helped by a boy employed at the inn, would have made one part as clean and comfortable as could be. "And [she] laid him in a manger, because there was no place for them in the inn" (Luke 2:7).

It's wild, really; yet the tremendous truth of Christmas is that in that "house," that stable, the baby born was God become man in a different, diviner sense than any other. It is so familiar now, with nativity scenes in our homes and churches and store windows. But it is still incredible to many intelligent people that God came in a baby, born of a woman, born under the law, not wafted through the skies but laid in a manger; not wrapped in luxurious blankets of the angels but wrapped in swaddling clothes; not hidden behind the great curtains in the secret places of the Temple but entirely devoid of the comforts of the inn, where only cattle rested and unheeding throngs hurried by.

It is dangerously easy not only to take Christ out of Christmas but to keep him forever as a baby in the manger. Musing on the baby Jesus, we may have nice pious, warm feelings and even think of the Lord of life and Savior of the world as "cute." Theologian Robert McAfee Brown's warning is necessary: "It is easy to gush over 'the baby Jesus' and what a sweet picture the stable scene makes on a Christmas card with 'cute little angels' flying overhead. We must not forget that the baby whom everyone

28

helps to adore will grow up to be the man everyone helps to crucify." [1]

Where to go at Christmas? Let God himself lead you home, to the house of Christmas, that you may find your sins forgiven and your sorrow and sighing lost in wonder, joy, and praise as you worship and adore the mighty God who came as a baby, grew to manhood, was tempted and tested in every way as we are, was betrayed and crucified, died for us and for all of God's children, was raised again from the dead, is forever at the heart of reality, the Friend of everyone, and the Lord of all life.

Where to go at Christmas? To a house that was no house and yet became the first home of our blessed Lord in whom is our ultimate hope of life, victory, and joy eternal. Is there another house? Yes, our own. We go to our own house. His grace, his Spirit, his unseen presence can make our house a true home. It may be that the house we live in is in an apartment, or one room, or a compact cottage — the first on which we've been able to make a down payment — or it may be a spacious house. No matter; where love is, God is. Where mutual love exists, a house, whatever its dimensions and design, becomes a true home.

Rudyard Kipling claimed that a house never lies. One's home is a fairly dependable indication of what he is. Christian traditions can grow. Traditions like reading the Christmas stories from the Bible during Advent and Christmas; customs such as listening to recordings of homespun carols or soaring classics, or making music around a piano or other instrument. One family I know doesn't feel that it's quite Christmas unless one of the circle reads aloud from Dickens' *A Christmas Carol;* another plays the recording of "The Littlest Angel," and then all who are old enough go to Christmas Eve Communion service in their church. They remember others and share their festivities with solitary folk, students, and others from other lands.

The home Joseph and Mary founded in Nazareth must have been a lovely home. We Protestants have shied away from making too much of Mary the mother of Jesus. As a result it is possible we have made too little of her and of her role in the life of her greatest Son. Mother, do you know that yours is the greatest job in the world? How strong and patient and under-

[1] Robert McAfee Brown, *The Bible Speaks to You* (Philadelphia: The Westminster Press, 1955), p. 118.

standing Joseph must have been! Recall from Luke's Gospel how Jesus in his twelfth year visited Jerusalem at Passover time. In the Temple he engaged, as intelligent Jewish boys would, in hearing and asking questions of the teachers. His parents knew panic for a little while; they thought he was lost. When they found him, Mary said, "Your father and I have been looking for you." Jesus responded, "Did you not know that I must be in my Father's house?" Gently but definitely Jesus takes the name *father* from Joseph and gives it to God. Was it then, with manhood dawning on him, that there came to him a sudden blaze of awareness that in a special sense he was the Son of God? No pride resulted. He went home with his parents, and the Gospel writer says he was obedient to them. A much-quoted sentence written by Luke telescopes the so-called hidden years at Nazareth into one memorable sentence: "Jesus increased in wisdom and in stature, and in favor with God and man" (Luke 2:52). "As Jesus continued to grow in body and mind, he grew also in the love of God and of those who knew him" (Luke 2:52, Phillips). In his own home Jesus related radiantly to the Unseen, with a happy naturalness. Is your home, is mine, one in which a child grows in trust of the gracious and loving God? Jesus must have been on good terms with most people. "He grew also in the love of God and of those who knew him." As a man it was inevitable that he would arouse opposition and at the end go down before deadly enmity. But it is a mistake to imagine that he antagonized everybody or even a large number of persons. Mark reported that "the great throng heard him gladly" (Mark 12:37). Would they have heard him so gladly if he had been a dour, somber person? He was a man of sorrows, but he was also a man of joy, welcomed at wedding receptions and able to romp with little children. When his enemies wanted to slander him, they exaggerated his zest for life. "Then the Son of Man came, enjoying life, and people say, 'Look, a drunkard and a glutton — the bosom friend of the tax collector and the sinner'" (Matthew 11:19, Phillips).

What of our homes? Is there mutual confidence, and love that never forgets or forsakes? The Italian patriot Mazzini was told that a certain person was a good man. Mazzini replied, "I don't know; I've never seen him at home." In the "intentions" drawn up by a group from the Society of Friends who were shaping a rule of life which they would follow together, there was one

30

significant commitment: "to share myself with my household (an hour daily in relaxed converse, such hours to be cumulative if a day was missed)." In Nazareth and elsewhere, Jesus gave himself greatly to those he loved. Do you? Do I?

Where to go at Christmas? To a house — *first, to a strange home in a stable,* irradiated by a light that never was on sea or land, where the Son of God was born; *second, to our own house,* even if we have no close family. *Then to the house — of God.* Shouldn't every house be a house of God? Yes; of course. Nevertheless, there is a sense in which the church makes a house a sanctuary. Correction: There is a *profound* sense in which God's people meeting together in his name, to realize together his presence and listen for his Word through Scripture, sermon, praise, prayer, and sacrament, find God himself making it his house. You are missing some of the most meaningful hours of life if you cannot say with the psalmist of ancient Israel: "O Lord, I love the habitation of thy house, and the place where thy glory dwells" (Psalm 26:8).

In spite of the commercialization and our secular ways, we know where we may go at Christmas to be at home with God who is our dwelling place in all generations.

"And the redeemed" — the found, the homesick, the strong, and the weak, who put their whole confidence in Christ — "shall come home . . . singing!"

PRAYER: Find us, O seeking Savior of us all; find us even when we are barricaded behind our love of security, even when we try to hide from thy love with its appeal for commitment to thy kingdom; yes, even when we try to escape thee in celebration of thy birthday. Come to us in our family joys and in our sorrows. Keep us from being both selfishly pagan and grimly pious, for we would rejoice that thou hast visited and redeemed thy people. Amen.

*Lead our minds and hearts to thy manger, Lord
Jesus. In thy holy incarnation may we be born
anew. Amen.*

WHERE TO GO AT CHRISTMAS?
TO A BIRTHDAY PARTY

SCRIPTURE: "The shepherds said to one another, 'Let us go over
to Bethlehem and see this thing that has happened, which the
Lord has made known to us.' And they went with haste, and
found Mary and Joseph, and the babe lying in a manger" (Luke
2:15-16).

A little girl attended her first Sunday church school Christmas
party. Her mother had carefully explained to her that it was the
celebration of Jesus' birthday. Evidently she expected more of
the party than what materialized, for when she came home and
her mother asked her how she enjoyed it, she said, with some
show of disappointment: "It was a nice birthday party, but Jesus
didn't come!"

Where to go at Christmas? To a birthday party! But it must
be a birthday party where Jesus is present. The greatest movement in history, the most beneficial and permanent revolution
this planet has witnessed, began with a birthday party. Correction: It all began in the far depths of God's being, for before
the world was, the Word — the presence of God — was. Nevethe-
less, as far as our planet and human history are concerned, it is
true that it began in a birthday party. The baby was born in the
strangest of maternity wards. If you and I had tiptoed in after
the reverent, humble shepherds, it wouldn't have seemed like
much of a party of any kind.

Children usually enjoy birthday parties. If you are very young
you enjoy most your own! For then you are on the receiving end
of the gifts. As you become more mature, your enjoyment of the
celebrations of others increases.

Where to go at Christmas? To the birthday party of Christ.
*Because we need to become "as little children" to receive the
greatest gift.* What is it to become as a little child? It is to have

a keen sense of wonder. Unless a child has been rejected or in some other way cruelly hurt, he has a natural capacity for wonder. Whatever the number of our birthdays, we have a need to be excited by the right events. It is true, as the late Halford E. Luccock put it, that the first effect of the coming of Christ ought to be that of lifting life out of itself into a joyful forgetfulness. Let's keep this motive power. It slips too easily out of our living. The best of us can become blasé — which means with the keen edge blunted. Our Christian religion is all centered in the glory which was at play in the coming of Christ into our world, into one human personality. Of an unusually beautiful sunset, a woman once said that it was a wonderful sunset for such a little place. A wonderful sunset can happen in any place. "Can any good thing come out of Nazareth?" the knowing ones asked when the baby born in Bethlehem had grown to manhood and begun his public mission. "Can any glory be born in Bethlehem?" they might have asked if the news of Jesus' birth had seemed important enough to tell anyone. What catches the breath with wonder is that God stepped into the need and despair and poverty of our world in a baby born to Mary in a village out there in the Middle East.

What a birth! What a birthday party the old stories sketch! Mother Mary, father Joseph, humble farm animals, a few curious, spiritually sensitive shepherds, and later, some dark-skinned, oriental — or perhaps African — stargazers.

Over a century ago a starchy, respectable New Englander living in Amherst, Massachusetts, made a proposal of marriage to a young woman. This man didn't believe in letting himself go. Ecstasy was a little too emotional, he would say. He told the lady that he had been evaluating her in his mind. He hoped that with some changes she might prove suitable to be his wife. He wrote: "I hope that I have no foolishness called romance; I am too well-balanced for that sort of nonsense. But we might look forward to leading respectable and useful lives and enjoy the respect of the neighbors." It would be interesting to know how many women here today would be swept off their feet by such a thrilling opportunity to lead a respectable and useful life! But this is the mood that can overtake our religious life if we let it dwindle down into routine, ritual, and respectability, and come to think that it consists completely of research and debate, and finding the most adequate intellectual concepts. We must be carried out of ourselves, and this cannot happen without feeling. Washington Irving called Christmas time "the season of regenerated feeling." A thoughtful, jolly Christian said that the true way to measure life is not by the number of breaths we take, but by the number of breaths we do not take when we are breathless in wonder and amazement. If only we could mean it to the depths of our souls when we sing:

> "Christ, by highest heaven adored,
> Christ, the everlasting Lord. . . .
> Veiled in flesh the Godhead see,
> Hail the incarnate Deity!
> Pleased as man with men to dwell,
> Jesus, our Immanuel!"

How Charles Wesley piled it on:

> "Light and life to all he brings,
> Risen with healing in his wings.
> Mild he lays his glory by,
> Born that man no more may die,
> Born to raise the sons of earth,
> Born to give them second birth!"

Today, and on Christmas Eve, and on Christmas Day, and in every week, we have to do not just with remembrance of a long-past historical event accompanied by familiar music. We are confronted by the very God himself coming in a real Person, Jesus Christ.

All this gives us the second reason for going to the birthday party of Jesus our Lord at Christmas. Do you remember how we reminded ourselves that commonly youngsters enjoy their own birthday party most because they are recipients of the guests' gifts? We, too, go to a birthday party — and it isn't ours — to receive the greatest gift. Here is giving in reverse. God's ways are not our ways. At this divine birthday party we learn that it can be more blessed to receive than to give. God so loved the world — not just the church, not just those of us who are in the majority group of our society — God so loved the world of persons that he gave us himself in the Son of his love, Jesus Christ. Love at its most extravagant is God's gift.

Have you ever had anyone rush up to you with good news? In a hospital a stranger excitedly says to you: "My baby's going to get better!" "My wife's temperature is normal!" "Johnny is coming home!" We, too, have glorious good news! God, the mighty God, called by so many names and all of them together not adequate: the Ground of Being, the Life Force, the Higher Power, the Father Almighty, Maker of heaven and earth — this infinite and eternal creator, redeemer, sustainer of life — has visited and redeemed his people in a human being born in a cattle shed, foretold in the secret Scriptures of the poor. He was born as you were born, as your baby was born; he was loved by his parents and by his brothers and sisters; he provoked resistance, hostility, hatred; he was arrested and executed. He was buried in a borrowed tomb. He was raised from the dead in some mysterious, tremendous manner. He is alive, within and among his own. All this was given *for* you and me; given *to* you and me, and all mankind, that we might be mended where we are broken; might never completely despair; might know that what should be at last shall be; that what is highest and best in man is deepest in nature; that beyond death's partings is reunion; that never again can it be completely night.

A piano teacher said to a pupil: "You seem to play the piano with a feather duster. You never strike down deep to the music that is in the instrument." How do we play our religion? I love the quiet music of serene trust: "Peace, perfect peace, in this dark world of sin," "Be still, my soul. . . ." There is God's peace subsisting at the heart of endless agitation. I like the tenderness of love, the love that passes knowledge, as you like it. But when I realize that in Jesus Christ God has come, and continues to come through the power of the Holy Spirit, to set his people free from self-despising, haunting fears, accusing memories, gnawing anxieties, and crippling guilt, I want to join in a fanfare of trumpets! You can't strike the deep notes of the music with a feather duster. How do you think the apostle Paul played the words "It is no longer I who live, but Christ who lives in me" or "Thanks be to God for his inexpressible gift!"?

We go to a birthday party not only to receive the unsurpassed gift of Christ himself. We go to bring gifts. One thoughtful church member said to me the other day: "Why not tell people they can put the church on their Christmas list? What about

36

gifts to the church, not only to make it more effective within our buildings, but to enable it to demonstrate that it cares . . . ?" After all, we are trying to love the world into newness of life — in downtown and in suburbs, in the fifty states and Puerto Rico, in Asia, Africa, and Europe. I keep wondering who brought to the family in Bethlehem milk and bread and honey, who helped Joseph to tidy up the stable, and who cooked the meals.

Do you know the lovely poem by Christina G. Rossetti in which she asks what we can give our Lord? She suggests that we give him our hearts! Will I? Will you? In commitment to the God he brings near? In renewed devotion to the persons and causes dear to his heart? At his birthday party all are welcome and all are present, just as at the last great party — what the Bible calls the supper of the Lamb — in heaven, all who love God and their fellow humans will be honored guests. Why are we sure? Because God is our Father; because whosoever will may come; because God has made of one blood all men; because God so loved the world, not just the church.

Where to go at Christmas? To a birthday party, the celebration of Jesus Christ's birth and life and death and resurrection; to recapture our first fine careless rapture; to let wonder lift us into self-forgetful joy; to receive the gift we can never deserve, even God's gift of himself, of his love, of meaningful life that is eternal; to give the gift he wants most of all — ourselves — given away to Christ, and *in* Christlike serving.

There's a hymn by Frances Ridley Havergal, two lines of which are:

"Take my hands and let them move
At the impulse of thy love."

There were hands, once a baby's hands in a crib, which moved for us finally to a cross. They were nailed there, at the impulse of God's love. The Christmas crib and Calvary's cross were both made of wood. Crib and cross are joined. A woman looked at the controversial statue of Jesus on trial by Jacob Epstein. Crude and strong, the statue shows Christ's hands tied. The woman cried with revealing simplicity: "If we could only untie the hands!" We can do it. We are called to do it. When we take hold of our world, of our job, of our chance to help with his love, we untie his hands.

PRAYER: In thy service, Lord, use me, simply, fully, freely. In thy power make me strong and in thy glory make me glad. In thy presence let me be now, and through eternity." Amen.

*As our thoughts move quietly to the manger
where Jesus was placed long ago, let the silence
of eternity be interpreted by love, O God.
Amen.*

WHERE TO GO AT CHRISTMAS?
TO A GENTLE STILLNESS

SCRIPTURE: "And after the earthquake a fire, but the Lord was not in the fire; and after the fire a still small voice" (1 Kings 19:12).

A sensitive writer has told a beautiful little Christmas story in which a small boy named David stood quietly for a moment in the snow in his backyard, looking up at the stars as they came out in a cold December sky. His mother had hardly ever seen him stand still. She slipped out of the kitchen door to be by his side. "All those stars," he said. "They shine so. But they don't make a sound." The mother saw in his wise, honest, little-boy eyes the miracle of an awakening soul. He stood awestricken for a moment. Then he whispered to her: "I thought I heard them singing . . . sort of."

Christmas stars do sing for hearts that are hushed to hear. To go to our spiritual Bethlehem, to travel star-led to the Christ child lying in a manger, is what we should do at Christmas.

When we come with the faith God gives us, in the grace that is in Jesus Christ, we come to a gentle stillness. It is with Christ, it is "in Christ" that we find the inner serenity and the peace which the world does not know and cannot give.

In the Old Testament story of Elijah, you remember that at the entrance of a cave the prophet experienced God unmistakably, unforgettably, and transformingly. Storm, earthquake, fire, but God was not in them. But "after the fire a still small voice." The phrase has been translated by James Moffatt: "After the fire the breath of a light whisper."

Valid also is the translation: "After the fire a sound of gentle stillness" (American Standard Version, variant reading).

Shepherds abiding in the field were accustomed to stillness.

The timid blat of a lamb, the low growl of a sheepdog, the distant rumble of thunder, the deep-spoken command of an alert watcher all accentuated the stillness.

But we are not shepherds. City life, even suburban life, has clamor. Boisterous voices and strident sounds mark our living. But at the first Christmas, silence must have been a prelude to the sounds of the celestial choir and a baby's cry. In the quietude of Bethlehem calm men were sent to greet the Christ.

Of course, there is a place for sound and songs, for bustle and good cheer, for carols and chiming bells.

We need to go to a place of gentle stillness so that we may grow in awareness of what is real, what is true, what is enduring, and what is lovely. Rudyard Kipling once paid tribute to three or four great military leaders he had known, stressing their unusual reserves of power and their capacity for creative quietness. You could make your own list: William the Silent, Wellington, Grant, Foch, Lee. Nor is this capacity found only in men of arms. Consider Tennyson in the eagle's nest of his favorite house; Goethe wishing he could built a Chinese wall around his inner self; Thoreau sequestering himself in the cool quiet near Walden Pond; Lincoln fleeing to the solitude of his deep purpose; Eisenhower finding retreat on a golf course. Charles Darwin stood for seemingly impossible lengths of time in his garden considering, reflecting, and seeking tirelessly for insight, and then, it is said, he emerged from that garden gate with an amazing truth, the harvest of a quiet eye.

When God revealed himself, not in a principle but in the most creative personality, he did so gently, through the Christmas silence:

> "O little town of Bethlehem,
> How still we see thee lie!
> Above thy deep and dreamless sleep
> The silent stars go by. . . ."

No crowds, no cheers, no clatter or tumult!

> "The world in solemn stillness lay,
> To hear the angels sing."

The most loved of all the nativity songs whispers of the peace of the manger room:

"Silent night, holy night,
All is calm, all is bright;
Round yon virgin mother and Child!
Holy Infant, so tender and mild,
Sleep in heavenly peace,
Sleep in heavenly peace."

When God launches a new planet; when he starts a new star wheeling through limitless space, he does so without the blaring of loud speakers. When God launched his Light of the world, the Light of life, in Jesus Christ, he did it so quietly that the Bethlehem folk slept through it. Only a few shepherds with quiet, attentive souls provided the audience.

"Hast thou heard God speak lately?" asked a Quaker of his companion. Then to the other's lowered glance, the questioner added, "Thou must have forgotten how to be quiet."

Let me change the question: Have you heard the joyous note of Christmas joy this year? No? Then after the bustle and feverish activity, take time to be quiet and hear what God the Lord will say. Let there be music and the sound of singing. But let there be also the voice of gentle stillness so that each of us may know that Christ is born, that our hearts, our homes, and our work may be the candle of the King. When we take the bread and the wine, let us believe

"How silently, how silently
The wondrous gift is given!
So God imparts to human hearts
The blessings of his heaven.

"No ear may hear his coming,
But in this world of sin,
Where meek souls will receive him still,
The dear Christ enters in."

PRAYER:

  O God,
Who art peace everlasting
  Whose chosen reward is the gift of peace,
And who hast taught us

41

That the peacemakers are Thy children,
Pour Thy sweet peace into our souls,
   That everything discordant may utterly vanish,
And all that makes for peace be sweet
   To us forever. Amen.

(Mozarabic Liturgy)

Bless now thy truth, O Lord. May thy love en-
lighten our understanding of thy Word. Make
and keep our hearts as altars of thy Word and
thy peace; in Christ. Amen.

WHERE TO GO FROM CHRISTMAS?
TO A CITY

SCRIPTURE: "By faith Abraham obeyed when he was called to go out to a place which he was to receive as an inheritance; and he went out, not knowing where he was to go. . . . For he looked forward to the city which has foundations, whose builder and maker is God. . . . They desire a better country, that is, a heavenly one. Therefore God is not ashamed to be called their God, for he has prepared for them a city. . . . For here we have no lasting city, but we seek the city which is to come. . . . But you have come to Mount Zion and to the city of the living God, the heavenly Jerusalem. . . . It [the city] had . . . twelve gates . . . on the east three gates, on the north three gates, on the south three gates, and on the west three gates" (Hebrews 11:8, 10, 16; 13:14; 12:22; Revelation 21:12, 13).

"Where to go *from* Christmas?" To a thrifty suburbanite the answer is obvious. To a city — to the city — to exchange gifts or purchases made for Christmas; to buy some of the goods offered in the post-Christmas sales! There are those who would differ. "Not for me," a weary survivor of the Christmas season might say. "You can have the city; I'll take the country; let it be some quiet spot where I can rest and recuperate."

When you ask the Bible where to go *from* Christmas, that is, from the fact that made Christmas, the Christ-event, the Incarnation of God in Jesus of Nazareth, the answer seems simple and clear. From Christmas you must go to the city. But when you ask what is meant by the term "city" the answer is not simple. In the Bible the word "city" is used many times. In Hebrew usage the word is used for almost any collection of permanent human habitations, many or few. It is also used metaphorically, as we sometimes use it, for the people of God. Thus in chapter eleven of the letter to the Hebrew Christians, they are reminded that they have come to "Mount Zion and to the city of the living God."

What of us? At the end of one year and on the threshold of a new year, where do we go from here? The Word of God speaking through the words of the Bible says that like all our predecessors we, too, are on pilgrimage. We are en route to the city of God. In the Book of Jeremiah we find some verses, beautiful within themselves, which tell of the agitation for the return of Jewish exiles from Babylon to their homeland: "They shall ask the way to Zion, with faces turned toward it, saying, 'Come, let us join ourselves to the Lord in an everlasting covenant which will never be forgotten'" (Jeremiah 50:5).

Is this more than poetry? If so, may we have answers to a few questions related to this affirmation? The questions are: *Why to a city? What city? What is the route to it?*

First, *why to a city?* Because a city means a community. A community is essential to living a Christian life. Indeed, without community it is doubtful that a human being can become fully human. Experiments of placing young children in isolation, the plight of those born without ability to hear or communicate, and the dreadful punishment of solitary confinement all indicate that under such conditions human beings either do not develop as personalities, or, if they have been normal before separated from a community, they tend to regress when they are isolated. The late Professor H. Richard Niebuhr of Yale University developed the symbol of what he called "trialectic" to indicate that the encounter of a faith never takes place in a vacuum. When a man responds to life's demands he always does so in a living context, which both colors his understanding of the demand itself and frames and supports his response. The Christian faith involves a three-way relationship: *God and man; God and the fellowship; man and the fellowship.* Without the triple character, the whole relationship tends to become abstract or mechanical.[1] In one of Hugh Walpole's novels, *Blind Man's House,* the blind hero almost wrecks the happiness of his home because of his pride and aloofness. He finally perceives what he has been doing and expresses it in these words: "I have learned this lesson of our interdepend-

[1] See Charles Duell Kean, *Making Sense Out of Life* (Philadelphia: The Westminster Press, 1954), p. 10.

ence. The lesson that all mankind now must learn. . . . No one of us can move any more — can sigh or sneeze, cough or whisper — without disturbing the rest of us.

. . . until we learn this fellowship — the fellowship, generous and understanding — of all living men on this earth . . . there will be no peace." [2] God has prepared for us a city, a community. God planned it that way. As William Morris said a century ago, "Fellowship is heaven, and lack of fellowship is hell."

What kind of city should we head for? The purely spiritual kind, which is possibly significant but to many practical persons, is ethereal, somewhat nebulous, and otherworldly? No, not exactly or exclusively. It is true that here in our mortal existence we have what the Bible calls "no continuing city." We are pilgrims and sojourners, as all our fathers were and as all human beings are. Nevertheless, he who knows not the city which he has seen cannot know, let alone love, the city he has not seen. A study book has the title *These Cities Glorious*. The cities to which the book refers are our American cities, and, of course, the author does not claim that all cities or even some of them are glorious in all respects. He is aware of much in the city that resembles a kind of fierce, man-devouring jungle. But he is sure that "Life in the city is not all graft and greed, delinquency and drunkenness, lust and low living. Nor is all life in the suburbs a complex mess of neuroses and psychoses, of status seeking and alcoholism." [3] He tells us what we should already know, that urban patterns have become characteristics of our entire society, both in city and country. He tells us that "the church, as the Body of Christ, has a tremendous responsibility not only to be at work in the city, but to make it 'the city glorious.'" [4] Therefore, as Christians in community, we are engaged continuously in mission to help God develop and transform our city into a community of disciplined, responsible, ethical citizens. It is too easy to say that this is the goal of Christians and other men and women of good will. It is swinging the Protestant incense: indulging in a glittering if noble generalization. Spelled out, it

[2] Hugh Walpole, *Blind Man's House* (Garden City, N.Y.: Doubleday & Company, Inc., 1941), p. 430. Reprinted by permission of Sir Rupert Hart-Davis.

[3] Lawrence H. Janssen, *These Cities Glorious* (New York: Friendship Press, 1963), pp. 9-10.

[4] *Ibid.*

involves effort, education, legislation, and persuasion on such fronts as urban renewal, better housing for all racial and economic groups, more adequate education for the increasing number of Negro Americans who are moving into our cities, and civic government notable for statesmanlike approach to problems and opportunities. To be a Christian on the way to a city glorious means to get mixed up in what we sometimes arrogantly call the dirty game of politics.

What then do the Bible and the Christian faith and ethic mean by looking forward to the "city which has foundations, whose builder and maker is God"? Abraham is said to have looked forward to such a city. He certainly could not foresee any visible city. When Abraham lived no one could envisage the city of Jerusalem of Solomon's time. But he did look to the future with the vision of faith. Josiah Royce, once a distinguished professor of philosophy at Harvard University, wrote: "I believe in the beloved community and in the spirit that makes it beloved, and in the communion of all who are, in will and deed, its members. I see no such community as yet, but nonetheless my rule in life is: act so as to hasten its coming." The Bible says: "By faith Abraham obeyed when he was called to go out to a place which he was to receive as an inheritance; and he went out, not knowing where he was to go. . . . For he looked forward to the city which has foundations, whose builder and maker is God." He had the faith that is ready to adventure. What would really happen to us, to a church, to the great church universal if we took God at his word and proceeded on his commands and promises? Bishop Lesslie Newbigin tells of the negotiations which led to the formation of the United Church of South India. He had a share in these negotiations. A former Presbyterian from Scotland, he was one of the United Church's first bishops. Referring to some discussion at the time of negotiation, he recalled the statement, "The demand to know where we are going is one which no Christian has a right to make." [5] It is not only true of Christians in India. Here in North America, here in this church, men and women of Christian faith frequently drive with the emergency brake on — just in case. We are often marked by a dull unadventurousness.

[5] J. E. Lesslie Newbigin, *A South India Diary* (London: SCM Press, 1951), p. 15.

"By faith Abraham, when he was called . . . obeyed; and he went out, not knowing whither he went . . . for he looked forward to the city which has foundations, whose builder and maker is God."

What kind of city do we wait for, and work for, and in adventurous but patient faith know that God will give to all who put their confidence in him and strive to do his work? The city of God is also a phrase to describe what we mean by "the kingdom of God." In the New Testament the city of God is the kingdom of God. It is the city which is to come, which has solid foundations because God is its architect and builder. It will be in reality what the best city merely foreshadows. God's people are waiting for this city, and they are on the march to it. Paradoxically, this city of the living God is one to which we *have* come; not that the kingdom has already come but that as members of the church founded on Jesus Christ we have already received proof of the kingdom. "You have come," says the New Testament. "You have come to Mount Zion and to the city of the living God, the heavenly Jerusalem."

What is this city like? In the last book of the New Testament, the book of the Revelation of the prophet John, there is a vivid, colorful picture of the city of God. In his vision of this holy and eternal city John doubtless owed some of the symbolism to the prophet Ezekiel. No one can say for certain what the symbolism meant to the writer. We cannot take this noble vision literally. The immense dimensions of the city seen by John tell us that there is room for everyone in this beloved community. It is foursquare, because in the ancient world the cube was the symbol of perfection. There is no temple there, because the entire city is itself the temple. Buildings do not make a church. Only the presence of God and of Jesus Christ make the church. In the perfect city no temple is needed, because God's presence is continually there.

Most interesting are the gates of the city of God. As John saw it there are three gates on each of the four sides. We do not know what John meant to symbolize by this arrangement, other than the universality of the church. There are twelve gates to the city of God. There is no one way, for there are as many roads into the kingdom as there are men to take them. As we are learning in these days of ecumenical councils and growing understanding, no church has the right to claim any monopoly on the way to God.

There is one symbolic interpretation of the twelve gates which John may not have imagined but which has meaning and beauty. The city has gates on each side. It is a picture of the ideal city; a picture of the ideal church. The gates are ever open and they face every direction from which the traveler may come.

The gates on the east — do they not stand for these people upon whom the sun is just rising, the children, the young men and women? They do not look for a shelter or refuge in their religion. They are not rebelling *against* the religion of their parents, for many of their parents had little or no religion. They seek a cause that can give meaning, purpose, and zest to life. Did not Christianity begin with a young man, the young Prince of Glory calling others who were young in heart to follow and to build?

On the north, three gates. The north speaks of cold, of bitter winds, and of storm, where a struggle and work are the order of the day. *You* may be in such a grim country now, but there strength for you is available. There will be rest in the storm for you, if not always *from* the storm. What the ancient people of God called cities of refuge are set up by God.

On the south, three gates. The south speaks of calm, sunny, blue skies, and of good fortune. There is danger in the south wind. Under it we may deteriorate. A man needs to take special care when he holds in his hands a full cup. When Sir George MacLeod, the founder of the Scottish community on the island of Iona, first visited southern California he was captivated by its lush citrus orchards and apparently ideal climate. He learned also that the average family income was higher than almost anywhere else. "It is all so sane and final here," he said to an American friend. "Sane?" was the reply. "Do you know there are more fancy religions in California than in all the states put together? Do you know there are more psychiatrists practicing here than in any other corner of the continent?" Without any smugness, is it not generally true that where the winds blow constantly from the south and the barometer seems permanently set at "fair" the land can become a wasteland, and the impressive cities can become cities of dreadful night? But on the south there is a gateway to God, too.

48

On the west, three gates. When we think of the west, at least symbolically, we think of the sunset trail, and those for whom the sun is setting and the shadows begin to lengthen. For the old, life can be lonely and empty. A mature Christian moving toward the western slopes of life's road developed an almost shattering fear of death and pain. One time when he was in a moment of deep sadness, Christ seemed to become intensely real to him and to say, "Let not your hearts be troubled. . . . In my Father's house are many rooms. . . . I go to prepare a place for you" (John 14:1, 2). "This," said the veteran Christian, "steadied me. I feel strong and safe now in the love of Christ."

There is one further question: What is the way to the city of God? Near the end of the second part of Bunyan's *The Pilgrim's Progress*, when Mr. Ready-to-halt got to the river, "the last words he was heard to say were, 'Welcome life!' So he went his way." On the west are three gates that lead to light and life. The gates are ever open. Where to go from Christmas? Where to go from where we are now? To a city whose architect and builder is God. To join in a covenant with God, to set your face toward the Zion to which he summons us. For people who say such things declare plainly that they seek a country, a homeland. . . . "Therefore God is not ashamed to be called their God, for he has prepared for them a city." A guide is better than a map, a hero is more satisfying than many maxims; his function is to enlighten and enhearten, to show what is possible and lure us to try. What other Guide, what other Hero, is there for us but him who said: "I am the way. Follow me"?

PRAYER: Eternal God, who hast called us to be pilgrims and pioneers, arouse in us an adventurous willingness to leave the past and to move forward with Christ to seek the city of God whose Builder and Maker thou art. Give us grace to dare bravely, to think wisely, to act resolutely, and by the power of thy Spirit to achieve triumphantly. We pray in the spirit and faith of Christ Jesus our Lord. Amen.

*Make a secret way into our souls, O God, and
come into them as truth and life and love, in
Christ. Amen.*

I BELIEVE IT!

SCRIPTURE: " 'If you can do anything, have pity on us and
help us.' And Jesus said to him, 'If you can! All things are possible to him who believes.' Immediately the father of the child
cried out and said, 'I believe; help my unbelief!' " (Mark 9:22-24).
" 'If it is at all possible for you, take pity upon us and help us.'
'If it is possible!' said Jesus. 'Everything is possible to one who
has faith.' 'I have faith,' cried the boy's father; 'help me where
faith falls short" (Mark 9:22-24, *The New English Bible*).
" 'If you can do anything, please take pity on us and help us.'
'If you can do anything!' retorted Jesus. 'Everything is possible
to the man who believes.' 'I do believe,' the boy's father burst
out. 'Help me to believe more!' " (Mark 9:22-24, Phillips).
" 'Have pity on us and help us, if you possibly can!' 'Yes,' said
Jesus, 'if *you* can! Everything is possible for the person who has
faith.' The father at once cried out, 'I do have faith, but not
enough. Help me!' " (Mark 9:22-24, *Today's English Version*).

New Year's Day is an appropriate time to move into the spiritual climate of affirmation. No one can find much nourishment
in a climate or on a diet of negations. Do you know the story
I have told others of the young woman whose rebellion against
people over thirty took the form of giving intellectual and emotional shock treatment to as many "squares" as she could? She
entered a confessional booth in a Roman Catholic church one
day, and started her statement by saying to the wise older priest,
"Father, I don't believe any of the things you believe or the
church teaches. I don't believe in God; I don't believe in Christ.
I don't believe in life after death, or in heaven or hell." When
she paused the father-confessor said, "My daughter, I did not
ask you what you do not believe. What do you believe?" "Well,"
she answered flippantly, "I do believe that two and two make
four." "Very well," said the priest. "Live up to that." I hope the

young rebel thought through some of the implications of living in a universe where two and two make four regardless of other factors.

At one time, a favorite colloquialism of our younger people was "Would you believe . . . ?" I wish to talk about the colloquialism: "I believe it!" These words will be used honestly and sincerely. There are many things I do not believe. I want to tell you of some of the truths I do believe. I recognize that there is an element of individualism in this credo, that it is much more important to know what the great church, the Christian community, believes than what I believe or doubt. But often we are tempted to wonder whether the official or full-time spokesmen of the church really believe what they say. Let me tell you what I believe, what seems to me to be among the essentials of a growing, dynamic, critical faith by which to live.

My mood now, and probably always, will be like that of the father of the unfortunate boy described in the Bible who had something which sounds like epilepsy. The boy was seized by violent convulsions. His father had brought him to Jesus' closest followers for a cure, or at least for relief, but they had been baffled and helpless. When Jesus learned of their helplessness, he said, "Bring the boy to me." Jesus then asked the kind of questions a physician would ask. The father answered, and then added, "Have pity on us and help us, if you possibly can!" "Yes," said Jesus, "if *you* can! Everything is possible for the person who has faith." The father at once cried out, "I do have faith, but not enough. Help me!" The familiar King James Version reads "Lord, I believe; help thou mine unbelief." Do not suppose that a Christian believer does not have doubts. One of my teachers was Dean Willard Sperry of Harvard Divinity School. In a platform discussion Dean Sperry was asked if it had ever occurred to him that the Christian religion might not be true. Dr. Sperry answered that it had certainly occurred to him, and that in fact he could feel that he really believed more firmly if at times he doubted.

First, *I believe that God is very much alive in his universe, in this world, in our lives.* Some gods are dead, and should be. You may recall seeing the cartoon in the *Saturday Review* for December 31, 1966, page 55, which showed a caveman making a huge, grotesque, fierce-looking statue. The caveman sculptor's wife is surveying the statue, which appeared to be some thirty feet high. Her husband is listening, holding his stone-age hammer and chisel in his hands. Mrs. Caveman is saying vehemently, "If you think I'm going to worship *that*, you're out of your mind!" Some concepts of the Ultimate Reality evoke the same response in me. God is infinitely greater than the best things men have said about him. Moreover, I am impressed not only by evidence of what a great astrophysicist, Sir James Jeans, called the Mind of a Mathematician in our universe, but our knowledge of one who deserves to be called the God and Father of our Lord Jesus Christ. A single increasing purpose appears to be operating in this cosmic field of operations. This purpose or design seems to include a tremendous experiment on our planet Earth. God seems to have initiated the experiment of seeing whether a species, the human species, can grow up from its lowly, crude beginning into mature men and women who will learn not only to tame the forces of nature and land on other planets, but also to live together in harmony, brotherhood, justice, and peace. Why do I believe in such a living Ultimate Reality? There are many reasons, not proofs. The chief one is that this Ultimate Reality has made himself known, has disclosed his character and purpose supremely in a person who lived and died in history, Jesus of Nazareth. The theological or technical word for this disclosure is revelation. To Christians, Jesus of Nazareth is the Lord and Savior Jesus Christ. A second powerful influence in my belief in God alive and at work is my own experience of his love and wisdom. Questions, some of them sharp, so far unanswerable, remain — questions caused by senseless pain, tragedy, and man's corruption. Lord, I have faith in you. I put my trust, my reliance in you. Give me more faith!

That Jesus Christ lived 1900 years ago in what we now call Jordan and Israel, that he was what those who knew him best said he was, that Christ is the key to the mystery of Ultimate Reality, and the one whom we must trust for being set free from guilt, fear, and spiritual death — this I believe. First of all, I believe that Jesus was human, completely human. He was no god or demigod merely masquerading as a man. He was born as babies are born and he grew up as every normal human being grows up. He knew what it was to be hungry, lonely, and poor; to be exhausted by hard work and by what people took out of him. He, too, experienced frustration, misunderstanding, and betrayal, and at the end (as an inner-city boy said) "He took the rap for us!" He died through a cruel miscarriage of justice. He needed and had friends, he went to parties, and he had to die.

But, in the second place, Jesus was more than the rest of human beings. Somehow God's presence and very self came through Jesus' personality, his words, his actions, his death, and his victory over death. No one has ever equaled him in bringing God near; no one has come near him. I am sure that God is love, love unending, love undiscourageable, love that will not let us go, because the love of God comes through what the New Testament calls the grace of our Lord Jesus Christ. Christ is what God has done for us to bridge the gulf between what we are and what we ought to be. Christ is God himself taking little short steps, so that we can keep up with him and be taken along by him into becoming sons and daughters, free, responsible, adequate, and forgiven. I believe, although I cannot frame an adequate theory about it, that Christ's life and death on a Roman cross set on a Jewish hill did for us what we could not do for ourselves. In the old hymn words:

"He breaks the power of reigning sin,
He sets the prisoner free."

I believe in the church as the body of Christ in today's world. I am troubled about many failures of the church to "get with it," to be relevant to today's needs, to champion the beaten and the broken, to be in the vanguard of the legions fighting for a Christian society in the world. I have moments when I might say with a cynic:

"Like a mighty turtle moves the Church of God.
Brothers we are heading where we've always trod.
We are not united, not one body we,
Not one in hope and doctrine, not even harmony!"

But I am not among those who write off the church as the so-called leprous bride of Christ. I believe that the great church, the holy catholic church, is integral to the Christian faith; that in a profound sense the early church father Cyprian spoke the truth when he said that outside the church (not the institutional expressions of the people of God, although these are inevitable and necessary) as the community of believers, the people of God, there is no salvation. Individual faith and obedience is one kind of thing; but individualism, or private, exclusively personal, religion is not Christianity. I believe that the church must be ecumenical, that Christ wills our unity, and that this unity cannot be fully and most creatively realized until we have organic union without uniformity. I believe that it is more than an epigram or cliché for us to affirm that only a united church can heal a divided world. I believe that in Christ's true and living church all are called to be ministers, servants of Christ. There are diversities of gifts and differing functions, but there is no double standard. Priests, pastors, preachers, missionaries, fraternal workers, and administrators of institutional Christianity are needed, whatever new structures are devised for the "establishment." But in Christ, in Christ's fellowship of the concerned, there is no division between laity and clergy except that of function and office. I believe that within the church the worship of God is the top priority and all else is derivative. I believe that the means of grace, the ways in which God's power comes to us so that we share it, are the sacraments, the preaching of the Word, the study of the Word, and the practical service of Christians in their several vocations. The church *gathers* for worship and study, for prayer and the sacraments, and it *disperses* into the world of Monday through Saturday. Wherever you are as a Christian — in classroom, laboratory, hospital, office, factory, military unit, home, playing field, party, theater, or wherever — there is the church.

I believe that God in Christ requires us to be involved in this world, that we must show our faith by our works. "Works" means much more than delivering baskets of goodies to underprivileged families at Christmas or any other time. Christian works include every concern of human beings for a full life; for instance, political reform, tutorial programs, interracial and intercultural planning, the crusade against war and violence, and the efforts to secure better housing for low-income citizens of every color and racial origin. The church must help to train and organize what are called the powerless, faceless people. Such groups must be of, by, and for the people. I believe that the more you and I are genuinely concerned for the betterment of our entire community, the more we are fulfilling our Christian mission. I believe that the Christlike love which unites invincible benevolence with justice is the resource and force we must use in our involvement.

I believe that every person — male and female, young and old — can experience the power and love and companionship of God and Christ as he exercises the faith and capacity to trust, and commits himself to this gracious God. I believe that we come by many different roads to God and to that realm which Christ called God's kingdom. But beyond all this I believe that we *can* and *must* come if we are to have life at its greatest. Change your mind, turn to the right, to the true, to the best you know. Turn your mistakes, your failures, and your sins over to God; he loves the burden. Accept God's forgiveness, trust God's knowledge of you rather than your knowledge of him, and live as if what Jesus taught was and is the truth. Do what you believe Christ would want you to do in your relationships and in your own situation, and you will have increasing assurance. Join the legion of the concerned, the company of Christ's followers. Keep your vision steadily on Christ. His servants may let you down, and fail you; Christ never will. I believe it! Try him.

I believe with the great church, that the gift of God to every-one who trusts him is life eternal. This begins and continues here and now, and it goes on forever. Flesh and blood will fail, but the real person, the personality, experiences resurrection. To me this is renewal of the essential spiritual life, the continuance of the personality, identifiable, developing, knowing, loving, willing. This next dimension of life is with the same communion of the saints, the soldiers of the common good who trusted in him and were not confounded.

PRAYER: Lord, we believe; help thou our unbelief. Lord, each of us has faith — some very little — none of us enough. Help us. Amen.

*Let thy light lead us, as it led men of old to
him who is the light of the world, even Jesus
Christ. Amen.*

HITCH YOUR WAGON TO THIS STAR!

SCRIPTURE: "The star which they had seen in the East went before them, till it came to rest over the place where the child
was. When they saw the star, they rejoiced exceedingly with
great joy; and going into the house they saw the child with Mary
his mother, and they fell down and worshiped him" (Matthew
2:9-11). "I am . . . the bright morning star" (Revelation 22:16).

"Hitch your wagon to a star!" was the directive Ralph Waldo
Emerson gave his generation over a century ago. It was his
way of telling them that everyone needs ideals, high standards,
and commanding purposes if he is to make the most of life.
More recently idealists and moralists have been saying a similar
thing when they ask us to aim high.

Today the Christian calendar brings us to a time and a word
which resembles Emerson's advice, but goes deeper and farther.
Today is the Sunday nearest the Feast of the Epiphany. As you
may know, this festival is far older than Christmas. Some think
that it may have been celebrated as far back as the first century.
In certain sections of the universal church it is called little Christmas. One of the events commemorated for many centuries on
the sixth day of January was the visit of the wise men to the
infant Jesus. As every child knows, they came because they
followed a star. The wise men were called Magi. The term is
difficult to translate. The ancient historian Herodotus said they
were originally a Median tribe. Medes were part of the Persian
Empire, and they once tried to overthrow the Persians, but their
revolution was a failure. Many Medes became teachers of
Persian kings; and often they became priests. Persians would
not offer a sacrifice to the gods without one of these wise men
present. Originally the term designated men skilled in philosophy, natural science, and medicine. They were seekers of the
truth. Remember, too, that everyone in that ancient world be-

lieved in astrology. They believed that the future could be foretold by the stars. They believed further that a person's destiny was settled by the star under which he was born. Superstitious people, those ancients! Judging by the columns in newspapers devoted to astrology, there seem to be a lot of them who are still around!

It is not hard to understand why the stars were assumed to have such power and meaning. People in the ancient world observed that the stars pursued steadfastly their appointed courses. Stars seemed to be orderly, dependable, and mysterious. If a brilliant star suddenly appeared, it looked to devout people as if God was breaking into his own order to announce some special thing. Thus the wise men in the birth story of Jesus were convinced that some heavenly brilliance was speaking to them concerning the entry of a king into the world.

Is it only a lovely legend? Isn't it the kind of thing that could easily have happened in that ancient world? Assume that modern astronomers' speculations are correct: that, as the associate curator of the Hayden Planetarium, Robert C. Coles, said, the light of the Christmas star could well have been caused by the conjunction of Mars, Saturn, and perhaps Jupiter. It is known that such an assembling of planets occurred about the time of the birth of Jesus. Certainly the tremendous truth and beauty did not spring from a myth woven of fancy in the pre-scientific world.

Today the Word of God comes to us bidding us not to hitch our wagon to the mysterious star the wise men followed, but with this summons: *Hitch your wagon, tie your life, to the greatest Star of all.* In the Book of the Revelation written by the prophet John, in the twenty-second chapter, Jesus is pictured as saying: "I am the root and the offspring of David, the bright morning star." Jesus is saying that in him is the fulfillment of the prophecy of Isaiah (11:1) and that he is at one and the same time the eternal source of being from which David came and the promised descendant of the famous king. Therefore, Jesus is himself God's chosen King. But what is meant by the claim, "I am the bright morning star"? To a Jew these words would revive many memories. To call a person a morning star would be to give him a very high rating. The morning star is the brightest of all. Rabbis said that Mordecai, the hero of the Book of Esther who vanquished the tyrant Haman, was a morning star. The title would also recall the great Messianic prophecy: "A star shall come forth out of Jacob" (Numbers 24:17). Jesus is the Star promised by God.

Today the word comes to us: *Hitch your wagon to this Star — Jesus Christ. Tie your life to his life. Commit your way to him.* Why should we? Haven't we outgrown Jesus of Nazareth, lovely as his life may have been, noble as his teachings doubtless are, heroic and sacrificial as his death by crucifixion was? Do we really need to link our life with the life of Jesus of Nazareth in some deep, inward mystical bond? Granted, we need his spirit, his ethic. Even the Bolshevists who established the Soviet Union admitted something like this. When they rejected religion they realized that one cannot maintain any society or state without morality.

But why isn't morality enough? Agnostics, non-Christian humanists, frequently are superior to Christian believers in their ethical attitudes and actions. Yet we discover that when morality is divorced from religion it tends to be little more than a matter of opinion. When you and I no longer believe in God, in the God and Father of our Lord Jesus Christ, we tend to slide out of every challenge, with the glib retort that what is right for you is not necessarily right for me. You know how we argue: "It all depends on circumstances, on environment, on heredity, and a whole host of complex factors over which no one has control."

Hitch your wagon to the bright and morning star — Christ — that you may have a star to steer by. One of the lilting songs of a few years ago, which may have come back into vogue again as a folk ballad, is one from the highlands of Scotland, "I know where I'm going and who is going with me." Do you? If there are no moral imperatives, if we reject the authority of Jesus Christ as Example and Savior, as Judge and Redeemer, it means that what Russia likes and what China likes is morally right for them, and what America likes is morally right for America. It means, too, that what John Doe likes is right for him, and if Jane Doe or Harry Doe likes something else, then *that* is morally right for them. Murdo Ewen Macdonald, a wise Christian, in *The Call to Obey* said: "Ethical relativism is the arch-enemy of integration of all levels of our existence." [1]

---

[1] Murdo Ewen Macdonald, *The Call to Obey* (London: Hodder and Stoughton, Limited, 1963), p. 21.

Perhaps one of our troubles is that you and I are confused about goals and about ways to reach the goals. We don't know where we are or where we're going. We may be in the same fix as the man on a transcontinental jetliner. He turned with an air of sophistication to the man beside him and observed: "This modern jet travel is amazing! Here I am going to Los Angeles, you're going to New York, and we're both on the same plane."

Jesus Christ is the bright morning Star to guide us into understanding of life's meaning and of our duty. Belief cannot long be separated from behavior. Creed and conduct are indissolubly united. Our immediate predecessors could pigeonhole Jesus as obsolete and any revelation of reality, such as divine, holy, righteous love, as unnecessary. They could, and usually did, live moral, unselfish, and ethical lives. But today? Every magazine or newspaper you pick up usually has an article on the slump in morality, private and public. Should we be surprised? After all, life has to be deeply rooted in the soil of authentic religion.

Link your life with this Star that you may have power. To link our lives with the bright morning star of Jesus Christ and his ethic of itself is not enough. Morality, even when it is based on religion, tells us what we ought to do, but it lacks the power to translate aspiration into actuality. Who wants to be bludgeoned with categorical imperatives till he is dazed and dizzy, and on the brink of despair? Men of the quality of St. Paul, Augustine, and Luther had powerful minds and strong wills, but the more they struggled against the primitive and animal drives within themselves the more they felt overwhelmed. The New Testament is neither a book on ethics nor a treatise on moral philosophy. It is a book that "from beginning to end proclaims a God who is able to bind up the broken-hearted, to set the captives free, and to lead those who sit in darkness. . . ." He is able to lead us into his own marvelous light. "Jesus Christ did not come into the world either to edify or to exhort — He came to save us from our sins. He is the power of God unto salvation to every one that believeth." [2] You may remember the little girl who needed to be adopted into a good home. She was lonely, unloved, and misunderstood. Her behavior irritated the matron of the home where she had been placed. Someone saw the little rebel, the little antisocial character, fastening a note which she had written

[2] *Ibid.,* p. 25.

on some shrubbery near the street. The note was brought to the matron, who read, with dismay: "To whoever finds this: I love you!" This is the message of the bright and morning Star. God came in Jesus Christ to tell us profoundly the same thing. The light shines in the darkness. Whoever sees that light — whoever comes to that light — knows that God loves him, that God sent the Son of his love to lead us out of the darkness of our self-despising, of our lostness, into his marvelous light. There can be no blackout of that light of God's love. "The light still shines in the darkness, and the darkness has never put it out" (John 1:5, Phillips).

Hitch your wagon to this Star. Link your life to this Life of lives, that you may know that God loves you with an unbreakable love.

Hitch your wagon to this Star that you may be guided into loving others into newness of life. What is meant by that radiant New Testament phrase? A life new in hope, new in courage, new in confidence, *new in lovingness.* "We love, because he first loved us" (1 John 4:19). "By this all men will know that you are my disciples, if you have love for one another" (John 13:35). Of course, it isn't always easy or simple to know how we should love another person without smothering or spoiling him. But anyone that keeps close to human need and to Christ gains insight.

A retired Baltimore schoolteacher was given a great celebration by former pupils on her eightieth birthday. She had taught in one of the worst sections of her city, and the change in the young people and families under her teaching in that neighborhood was noteworthy. Many of the pupils became good citizens, some of them leaders in useful professions. In an interview she was asked what was her secret. She replied, "Oh, I don't know. When I look at the young teachers in our schools today, so well equipped with training and learning, I realize I was ill-prepared to teach. I had nothing to give but love." Nothing but love! Is there anything greater to give? It is the love which, as the Bible says, "is slow to lose patience — it looks for a way of being constructive. It is not possessive: it is neither anxious to impress nor does it cherish inflated ideas of its own importance. . . . It is not touchy. It does not keep account of evil. . . . On the contrary, it is glad with all good men when truth prevails" (1 Corinthians 13:4-8, Phillips). When we have fellowship with the Father and with his Son Jesus Christ such love grows.

Hitch your wagon to this bright and morning Star. Link your life through trusting faith and commitment to the God who draws near us in Jesus Christ. You will be a wise man, a wise woman, *you will have the Star to steer by, and know the way you should take. You will have the power of God in his love to enable you to do and be what otherwise you couldn't. You will be guided into doing something about it.* Therefore you, too, will see the Star by day and by night, and rejoice with exceeding joy.

PRAYER: Help us, O God, to arise and shine in the knowledge that thy light has come, and thy glory has risen upon us. When darkness covers the earth enable us to behold thy glory which knows no blackout. Manifest Christ in our time through the love and power of the Christian church, the vision of Christian scholars, teachers, writers, dramatists, artists, men and women in industry and business, in education and in science, beginning with us; in the grace of Jesus Christ the light of the world, and our Savior. Amen.

*Give us, Lord, clear vision of the truth, trust in
thy power, and confidence in thy love. In
Christ's name, Amen.*

YOUNG AND FOOLISH?

SCRIPTURE: "Let no one despise your youth, but set the believers
an example in speech and conduct, in love, in faith [loyalty],
in purity [sincerity]" (1 Timothy 4:12). "Don't let people look
down on you because you are young; see that they look up to you
because you are an example to them in your speech and behavior,
in your love and faith and sincerity" (1 Timothy 4:12, Phillips).
"We are fools for Christ's sake" (1 Corinthians 4:10).

"Let no one despise your youth." They may not despise your
youth, but they certainly criticize it! Doubtless the more philo-
sophical young people write off much criticism because they
know that it is characteristic of age to be shocked or annoyed
by youth. The list of indictments of youth's attitudes and actions
is formidable. Consider a few. You drive too fast. You want the
car too often. You stay out too late (or rather too early) too
often. You date too young. You go steady long before you should.
You marry too soon.

You young people are accused of being conformists. To what
do you, or to what are you supposed to, conform? To the aims
of upper-middle-class American society. When it comes to choos-
ing a life vocation you have learned from your elders that
so-called great rewards in our society go to the leaders of business, industry, and finance. We are told that colleges and uni-
versities produce too few writers, teachers, social workers, ministers, artists, and dramatists because the colleges have become
oriented to the dollar sign and to the life of the organization man.
Arthur Koestler believes that you are a new breed, an earnest,
bland, sober set of people, inscrutable, and with no strong con-
victions. A contrary opinion concerning at least a minority of
those in college is found in a *New York Times Magazine* article
by Harold Taylor, former president of Sarah Lawrence College.

His title expresses his thesis: "The New Young Are Now Heard: A generation is emerging which asks of its elders, 'What do you know? What can you do?'"

In June, 1960, I was at the Ecumenical Institute in Bossey, near Geneva, Switzerland, engaged with other pastors and professors in study of the church's mission in today's crisis-ridden world. One of the staff of the Institute, Dr. Charles C. West, is a graduate of Yale University. Knowing of my interest in that University, he loaned me his copy of an alumni publication. In it an undergraduate evaluating his own generation wrote:

"We are the antiseptic generation. We have grown up protected from the germs of extremism which had given our elders a case of intellectual gout. For us, history is a study only of the past; greatness today is not our necessity. Therefore we concentrate on 'life adjustment,' which helps us rid ourselves of the little idiosyncrasies of which greatness is made. Malcontentism is as great a sin as adultery and probably more often punished. But somewhere in the back of our minds we know that this protection is but a flimsy wrap. We want to know more, hear more, do more, think more, but our society neither encourages nor rewards those who inquire."

I read that statement in the study center of the World Council of Churches where all the menial labor was being done by young women of several countries, only a year or two younger than the college man who wrote the evaluation of the "antiseptic generation." These girls are called "blue angels," not because they are either depressed or completely angelic, but because they wear blue smocks as they wait on tables, wash dishes, prepare meals, and clean the dormitory and classrooms. Each of them almost fought for the opportunity to serve in the ecumenical studies center for at least a four-month term, without salary. They are given a small allowance for pocket money. From Europe, Africa, and North America they came. Why? Because, within the Christian context, they wanted to know more, to hear more, and to think more about how the complex issues of the world we have made may be handled without limited or unlimited war, or submission to any totalitarian tyranny.

In every high school and on every campus there is at least a significant minority of young people who with their sophistication and skepticism have hardheadedness and concern about making our world more just, peaceable, and fraternal. Young and foolish? Yes, undoubtedly many young people would acknowledge that they are and have been so, even as we their predecessors were once young and foolish. What disturbs us older people is that too often the young generation imitates our vices instead of the few virtues we may still retain. Certainly the adjective "foolish" applies to more than the generation now in their late teens and early twenties. You are young, and certainly it is no crime but a distinct advantage to be young in our nation today. No longer does a national leader need to say, as did William Pitt, the great Earl of Chatham, in the House of Commons: "The atrocious crime of being a young man . . . I will neither attempt to palliate nor deny." Indeed, the reverse was true when we had John F. Kennedy as president, one of the youngest men ever to lead a great nation.

Do you remember the story that went around while President Kennedy was in office? A White House guard is reported as yelling: "Hey! You kids, get off the lawn. . . . Oh, excuse me, Mr. President!"

You are young, and we envy you your youth. What oldster does not wish he could be around to see what you will see in the next fifty years? Older persons have always been tempted to look down upon the young. It must have been so when St. Paul wrote to his junior colleague: "Let no one despise your youth." Timothy was not a child. The word translated "youth" is a Greek word used to describe any one of military age, that is, up to the age of forty. The church always preferred to choose officers from among the middle aged and those whom we now euphemistically call "senior citizens." One organization manual of the early church, *The Apostolic Canons,* laid down the rule that a man was not to become a bishop until he was over fifty. By then, said the book, "he will be past youthful disorders." Those churchmen of long ago were optimists! Timothy was young when compared to Paul, and Paul knew that many would watch Timothy critically, ready to pounce on him for any error or shortcoming.

Are you foolish as well as young? Being honest, many of you would confess to a contemporary or to a trusted older confidant that you frequently are foolish. We, your immediate ancestors, need to confess to you that one of the major reasons for the young being foolish in their moral experimentation and their reluctance to support causes we have learned to value is due to us. Without selling America short, it is true to say that American society is widely and deeply unchristian in many of its features and standards. Many of us are hollow, confused, and without direction or purpose. Young people are not responsible for the culture in which they have grown up. Their world is not one which they made. But, thank God, the world of today and tomorrow is one which, under God, they can help to remake. We pray that you younger people may not repeat the tragedy of Rip van Winkle. Some wise man observed that the real tragedy of Rip van Winkle was not that he deserted his family for drink but that he slept through the American Revolution with a loaded gun and never fired a shot for freedom. Any young person who follows Christ commits himself to Christ's pattern of personal and social living and will never sleep through the global revolution now proceeding.

Paul gives Timothy advice. Most of us, certainly in my age group, have much advice to give young people. I have a large quantity, because I used up so little of what I was given when I was young! Paul's advice, however, is worth receiving and using:

"Don't let people look down on you because you are young; see that they look up to you because you are an example to them in your speech and behavior, in your love and faith and sincerity."

Paul is asking Timothy to accept one of the toughest assignments. He knows that arguments cannot silence criticism. We must live the life which demonstrates that our folly is essentially wisdom.

First, demonstrate your love. Love. There's a word, if you ever heard one, that is in need of a rescue party. The hit songs, Hollywood films, television plays, and popular fiction, have almost persuaded us that love is exclusively a sentimental, romantic, or biological experience. Real love includes all three of these elements, but the love of which Paul is writing is something deeper, higher, and wider. He speaks of *agapē*, using the Greek word for the greatest of all Christian qualities and forces. One scholar, Dr. William Barclay, feels that while this word is almost untranslatable, the nearest meaning is "unconquerable benevolence." If any one has this kind of love, no matter what other

66

people say of him, do to him, or how they treat him, he will seek nothing but their good. This is the love which we recall when we think of Jesus our Lord on the Cross, loving his crucifiers whom no man could *like*, and praying for the best for them. Such Christlike love requires superhuman assistance if we are to succeed in having it. This love enables a person of any age to go beyond the call of conventional morality or duty. It is said that love is something you do. Let us in our words and in our conduct, show ourselves as examples of love.

The second target Paul set for Timothy is *faith* or *loyalty*. Loyalty is perhaps the most accurate term to use in this sentence. Certainly there is a direct connection between faith and faithfulness. For the Christian it means invincible fidelity to Christ. A partisan is not neutral, nor is he lukewarm in his allegiance. We are partisans of Christ. When the situation is, as we say, really rough, it is hard to be loyal. When the situation seems hopeless, and we are in the midst of a campaign we cannot understand, then, as true soldiers, we remain steady in our loyalty. We trust our commander, believing that he knows the objective, the strategy, and the tactics. With such loyalty to the God disclosed in Jesus Christ, we remain constant in our loyalty to our companions who are in the same service. We do not despair of persons, nor do we grow cynical about the value or potential of individuals. Julia Ward Howe once held a reception for the eminent actor Edwin Booth. She invited the Senator from Massachusetts, Mr. Charles Sumner, to attend. She told the Senator that she wished him to know Mr. Booth. The Senator said that he didn't know that he cared to know Mr. Booth. Mr. Summer said that he had outlived his interest in individuals. Later, recalling the remark, Julia Ward Howe said, "Fortunately God Almighty has not, by last accounts, got so far." No one who is loving and loyal in Christ ever gets that far.

The third objective Paul set for his young friend may be translated *sincerity*. Some of the "beat" comedians have caricatured the tendency of many of us to excuse any performance by any person on the grounds that at least the person was sincere. In one's profession and in his relationships with others it is not enough to be sincere in this thin sense. The adjective "sincere," as used by Paul, comes from a word meaning "lean, pure, sound; *genuine*." It means that we are committed to Christ and his cause. To his way of thinking of reality, of ourselves, of others, of our duties as citizens of our country and of the world we are genuinely committed. When the heat is turned on we do not retreat or dissolve in facile, false adjustment. An early Roman governor named Pliny made this report about the Christians in Bithynia to his Emperor, Trajan: "They are accustomed to bind themselves by an oath to commit neither theft, nor robbery, nor adultery; never to break their word; never to deny a pledge that has been made when summoned to answer for it."

The Christian pledge was to a life of genuine honesty, honor, discipline, and consideration of others. You are young. Are you foolish enough to be fools for Christ's sake? You are facing a dangerous world, but it is God's world. There are continuing problems to solve. Are you foolish enough to commit yourselves to the fortifying faith of Christ, the commanding cause of a more Christlike international society, and the creative fellowship of Christ's church around the earth? Have you courage enough? One of the great Americans of the century is James Thurber who made so many see life's lighter side although, almost blind himself. In his appreciative biography of his former chief, the late Harold Ross, founder and first editor of *The New Yorker*, Mr. Thurber said: "He sometimes threatened to quit, and he was at least twice threatened with being fired, but he kept on going like a bullet-torn battle flag, and nobody captured his colors and nobody silenced his drums." [1]

I think we older people want this for you, that when you feel like quitting, when you feel your future is threatened by forces too powerful to subdue, you will have the faith and loyalty, the love and genuineness to keep going "like a bullet-torn battle flag." We pray that nobody may capture your colors or silence your drums.

PRAYER: O God, whose Son Jesus Christ was the young Prince of Glory, grant thy grace to every young person that each may come up to the gates of dawn, loving, loyal, genuine in their concern for what matters, because each is captured by Christ's dream of a world redeemed, found in the secret Scriptures of our faith. Amen.

[1] James Thurber, *The Years with Ross* (Boston: Little, Brown and Company, 1959), p. 309.

Make us able, Father of us all, to think in thy
wisdom, to speak in thy truth, to live in thy
love, through Jesus Christ in whom we all are
one. Amen.

BEYOND DESEGREGATION

SCRIPTURE: "For he is our peace, who has made us both one, and has broken down the dividing wall of hostility" (Ephesians 2:14). "But now in union with Christ Jesus you who once were far off have been brought near through the shedding of Christ's blood. For he is himself our peace. Gentiles and Jews, he has made the two one, and in his own body of flesh and blood has broken down the enmity which stood like a dividing wall between them" (Ephesians 2:13-14, *New English Bible*).

At a national conference on religion and race, Mr. R. Sargent Shriver, Jr., then U.S. Peace Corps director, said, "As a layman I wonder how I can go to church 52 times a year and not hear one sermon on the practical problems of race relations." Mr. Shriver is a member of the Roman Catholic Church. His question does apply to other churches as well as his own. It may be that the church which Mr. Shriver attends is one of a minority within the Roman communion. It may be that there are only a few Christian churches, Roman or Protestant, that never speak of the practical problems of race relations. In any case when today we think together of going beyond desegregation in the church, we speak not from any posture of pride. It is also true that in the United Presbyterian branch of the holy catholic church, to which I belong, the majority has long since declared that segregation is not only against the law of the nation, but is a sin against God and man. Nevertheless, no one who knows and loves the church may deny that repeatedly we have sinned against what we know to be God's truth and God's will in our relationships with those of other racial backgrounds. More than one expert in the field of race relationships has said that in the area of race the world has left the church behind. Dr. Kyle Haselden, editor of *The Pulpit*, wrote, "There has been more race relations progress in the civic, social, occupational, judicial and recreational areas of American life than there has been in the religious areas and in the church." On this Race Relations Sunday the church must speak faithfully to the nation. "The racial problem has been and continues to be this nation's oldest, most tenacious and most pervasive domestic problem. Before the white man had been 70 years resident in this country he had enslaved the Negro, justified this slavery in his laws, undergirded his enslaving laws with theological notions and moralistic sentiments which labeled the Negro inferior and cited God as the justifier of slavery, and, not incidentally, had discovered that enormous material gain could be had by holding human beings in chains." [1] Dr. Haselden went on to say that because of our human pride, greed, and fear we tend to hold on to these patterns. Therefore the church must speak to the citizens of this nation, but its people must speak in a mood of repentance for their own grievous sins. We cannot speak from any righteousness we have achieved. Martin Luther said that the countenance of the church is the countenance of a sinner.

What word of God can be said to ourselves and to our fellow citizens on what has been called our number one domestic problem? One word of God comes through the words of the Bible written in the letter to the Ephesian Christians: "For he is our peace, who has made us both one, and has broken down the dividing wall of hostility." Originally this statement referred to the division between Jews and Gentiles in the early church. The division was then partly racial, but more largely religious. This division has long been closed. A famous conference in Jerusalem, that today we could call an ecumenical council, settled the matter. You may read about it in the fifteenth chapter of the Book of Acts. Certainly the last fifty years have seen the ecumenical movement break down many walls which formerly separated Christians from one another. In passing it is interesting to note that in ecumenical meetings, either of the World Council of Churches or of the Pope's Vatican Council, there is little if any evidence of discrimination on grounds of color, nationality, or race. I wish this could be said of the church at the level of every local congregation. "Men often hate each other because they fear each other and they fear each other because they don't know each

[1] Kyle Haselden, *The Pulpit* (February, 1963), p. 3.

70

other and they don't know each other because they fail to communicate with each other, and they don't do that because they
are separated from each other," wrote Dr. Martin Luther King.
How can we bridge the gulf, cross over the barriers? It is hard
for us to believe that Christ whom we reverence and even adore
is really our peace. Christ, says the New Testament writer, is
like a greatly loved and respected friend who comes into a fierce
quarrel between two persons. Both of these opponents love the
third person. He talks to them, brings their hearts and hands
together, so that there is every chance of breaking down the
hostility which separates them. When two parties quarrel, the
surest way to bring them together is through someone whom they
both love. That is what Christ does. *He* is our peace. It is in a
common love for him that people of different cultures, back-
ground, appearance, and customs come together. "But now
in union with Christ Jesus you who once were far off have been
brought near through the shedding of Christ's blood." The
peace is won at the price of his blood, for the great awakener
of love is the sacrifice of God's loved Son on the cross.

Does this word provide direction so that we as Christians and
as human beings may go beyond desegregation? I believe it does.

First, *let us accept the fact that segregation of the Negro is
coming to an end.* One hundred years ago President Abraham
Lincoln proclaimed the emancipation of the Negroes. But only
in 1954 did the Supreme Court of the United States pronounce
segregation constitutionally dead. A noble Christian commenting
on the court's action declared: "Even the devout diehards who
used to cry 'Never' are now saying 'Later.' Much of the tumult
and the shouting . . . represent the fanatical death-throes of a
dying system. . . . I am convinced that in less than ten years
desegregation will be a reality throughout most of the South."
Desegregation has made great strides. But for Christians and for
Americans of every religious faith and of none, one powerful
fact must be faced. "However, when the desegregation process
is 100% complete, the human relations dilemma of our nation will
still be monumental unless we launch now the parallel thrust of
the integration process." [2]

"What more are you doing than others?" asked our Lord. We

[2] Martin Luther King, "The Ethical Demands of Integration," in *The
Presbyterian Outlook*, Vol. 145, No. 4, p. 5.

must go beyond desegregation and even beyond actual integration. Desegregation is the first step to the good society. Integration as a positive acceptance of desegregation is the next step, and a most important one. It means that Negroes will be welcomed as participants in the total range of human activity. But after that? Let a Southerner and Christian give the answer. He is Professor James Sellers, a professor of Christian Ethics and Theology at Vanderbilt University Divinity School, in Nashville, Tennessee. Before his academic career he was a newspaper editor in Northern Florida near the border of Georgia. He writes: "When I say white and Negro must now become better neighbors, I mean, quite simply, that we must learn on both sides how to treat each other as human beings. Let us not confuse what I am asking — human encounter — with a counterfeit sentimentality. If segregation will no longer work, if justice steeped in hostility is not a solution, neither will artificial togetherness produce neighbors," writes Professor Sellers. "What can create neighbors, though, is to learn to respect and live with each other as men." [3]

Listen also to another Southerner, James McBride Dabbs, Presbyterian elder, South Carolinian, plantation owner, grandson of a Confederate warrior: "The desire for justice among both Negroes and white is growing stronger in the South. . . . The fact remains that we are more concerned than our fathers were how to live together in the world. It may be because it is becoming more difficult to live together in the world. . . . Perhaps we have built, all unintentionally, a world which demands that we follow more closely the Judeo-Christian tradition." [4]

This is going to be a tough assignment for both whites and Negroes. One astute observer, Francis Pickens Miller, points out that "a new and more ominous kind of segregation, that of the mind and spirit is consciously practiced by members of both races against each other." [5] How can we overcome this psychic separation between races even in the midst of efforts to remove the barriers of law and custom?

We can take our Christian ethic seriously. How can we do

[3] James E. Sellers, *The South and Christian Ethics* (New York: Association Press, 1962), p. 9.

[4] James McBride Dabbs, *The Southern Heritage* (New York: Alfred A. Knopf, Inc., 1958), pp. 248-249.

[5] Sellers, *op. cit.*, p. 153.

that? It is good and necessary to ask: On what grounds should Christians take their stand in race relations?

We should know the *political grounds*. As the governor of South Carolina told his fellow citizens in that State, when the Supreme Court of our nation has spoken it is our duty as responsible citizens to obey it. When our Congress enacts a law we must support it, whether we like it or not. If we think it is unjust we may work to change or repeal it. An elemental necessity for civil order is that we support the due processes of law.

The *sociological grounds* for ending segregation, the ghetto pattern of life, for any group of Americans should be plain. Can a democracy exist for long when any group of people within it are second-class citizens? Moreover, on grounds of facing the facts of life in this interdependent world, how we treat each other in the United States speaks more loudly than anything we say in the Supreme Court, in our pulpits, in our newspaper editorials, or in the billions we have spent in assistance to struggling peoples in Asia and Africa and Europe. Here is a statement that leaped at me from a printed page: "If the world were reduced to a thousand people, there would be 303 whites and 697 nonwhites." [6]

To a fashionable Back Bay, Boston, audience, a Negro speaker said, "Your ancestors came over in the Mayflower. My ancestors came over in a slaveship. But we are all in the same boat now." This is one world.

It should not be difficult for us to recall the *ethical grounds* of our position (or what should be our position). Standing in the succession of the great Hebrew prophets and going beyond them, our Lord commanded us to love God and to love our neighbor as we love ourselves. This means that we give our neighbor, whoever he may be, the same rights and opportunities that we claim for ourselves. As Dr. Samuel McCrea Cavert wrote, "To establish segregation by color or class is to do violence to the human spirit in a way which cannot be justified by anything we have learned from Christ. A young clergyman in Oxford, Mississippi, gave a forthright, concrete example of this Christian ethical factor when he said to a rioting mob a few weeks ago: 'None of us can stand in the presence of Jesus of Nazareth, look

[6] Bruce Evans, "A Voice from the South," *Pulpit Digest* (February, 1963), p. 40.

Him squarely in the eye, and say that a Negro should not be admitted to the University of Mississippi.' " [7]

Valid and binding on anyone who lives in the Hebrew-Christian tradition, there is a deeper level even than the ethical. This ground is the foundational Christian faith. No one can long submit to his own prejudices easily who realizes that our attitudes toward other human beings are derived from two basic doctrines of the church.

First is the doctrine of creation. According to this belief, humanity is one. Mankind has a common origin in a sovereign God. In the Old Testament the origin of man is traced back to a common origin in two creation stories in Genesis having Adam and Eve as the figurative prototypes of all men. Dean Liston Pope of Yale University Divinity School tells of a rabbi who was asked why God created only two people in Genesis. The rabbi replied that it was so nobody could say, "I come from better stock than you do." God created man in his own image, in his spiritual likeness. God placed man on earth, pulling him and pushing him by the wonderful processes of evolution until he could live responsibly in obedience to his Creator. Man — every man — has a sanctity, a sacredness, a worth, not in himself primarily but in the very source of his being — God. In the New Testament this truth is expressed in various ways. In Athens, perhaps facing listeners of many different nationalities with many prejudices, Paul declared: "And he made from one every nation of men to live on all the face of the earth" (Acts 17:26).

A British soldier went through the terrible ordeal of Dunkirk in World War II. If any defeat can be glorious, the defeat of Dunkirk was glorious. When he was safely back in England a friend asked him, "What did it feel like out there on the beach at Dunkirk, with the sea in front of you, the German army behind you, and the German bombers overhead?" The soldier answered: "It was a strange feeling I had. I had the feeling that every man on the beach was my brother." The gospel of Christ says that not only every man on the beach but every man in the world is our brother and every woman is our sister. Have we not all one God for our Father?

For the Christian there is even stronger ground on which to

[7] Samuel McCrea Cavert, "The Gospel and Race," *Pulpit Digest* (February, 1963), pp. 7-8.

stand on behalf of going beyond desegregation. It is the *doctrine of redemption.* Somehow in the life and particularly in the sacrificial death of Jesus Christ, something was done for us that we could not and cannot do for ourselves. God was in Christ — in Christ in his dying and undying love, reconciling the world to himself. It was not the world of white Protestants or white Roman Catholics or white people generally. "God so loved the *world* that he gave his only Son." Christ has died for all. All have equal worth in God's sight. Moreover, in Christ, as St. Paul insists over and over, there is the beginning of a new humanity. This was expressed by the eminent biblical scholar J. A. T. Robinson when he said, "The fact of the new man is the very Gospel itself." This new creation begun in Christ "embraces potentially the whole human race. . . . The Church is the first-fruits of the new creation." In this new creation the old separations fall away. The walls come down. The barriers fall. "You who once were far off have been brought near through the shedding of Christ's blood." In this new creation there "cannot be Greek and Jew . . . barbarian, Scythian, slave, free man, but Christ is all, and in all" (Colossians 3:11). "With us therefore worldly standards have ceased to count in our estimate of any man. . . . When anyone is united to Christ, there is a new world; the old order has gone, and a new order has already begun" (2 Corinthians 5:16, 17, *The New English Bible*).

See what serious implications this truth has: Whenever we discriminate against any person or group because of race or class, we deny Christ's work in the world. We act as if Christ had died in vain, as if God's love was a lie.

Do you ask "Then why can't we wait until God's Spirit of love changes the hearts of a majority? Why try to legislate better race relations?" No one can coerce love in another. We do not secure neighborliness by law. But the biblical basis of better relations includes justice as well as love; justice, as a sign of love. It is important to remember that "the worst effects of injustice *can* be minimized by pressure and legislation." [8] When the armed forces were integrated racially, the new policy did not work a miracle in changed relations. "But many Southerners, led into close contact with the Negro through this pressure, learned to see him for the first time as man endowed with rights and . . . be-

[8] Sellers, *op cit.,* p. 162.

ing capable of fellowship. In short, the silliness of segregation became obvious."[9] God is not only loving but concerned with justice. Reinhold Niebuhr thinks that we may well have to start with the securing of justice if we are able to love our neighbors at all.

Is this enough? No. Justice alone is never enough to carry out God's purposes or even to create a sound society. We must go the whole way with the word of God. Judgment begins at the house of God. So does neighborliness. What does this imply? It is almost impossible to spell it out in advance. *But would you not agree that a minimum of neighborliness requires us to worship together?* True, Negroes often do not wish to worship with us, do not wish to come to our churches. That is not the point. The point is whether or not they feel welcome. Dr. J. Claude Evans, chaplain of Southern Methodist University, Dallas, Texas, tells of a South Carolina friend who considered himself a segregationist. Asked what he would do if a Negro walked into his church and took a seat beside him, the Southerner thought for a moment and said, "I'd offer him a hymnbook." When such an act of Christian obedience happens, abstractions about race collapse.

Once a college dean, Dr. Lynn Harold Hough, called the roll of his class. He came to the name of Harry Robinson. Harry wasn't there. Trying to establish Harry's excuse, a pal of Harry's spoke up. "Dean, Harry can't be here today. You see, he is getting married." Without looking up the Dean cracked back, "Interesting, but irrelevant."

When the roll is called up yonder and you and I stand before the God of all, claiming special consideration because of our self-built feelings of superiority, we might say, "We've been faithful Protestants, or good Catholics, or loyal Republicans, or hard-working Democrats, brilliant scientists or liberal educators, or successful executives or conscientious ministers, or white Americans, or Negro Americans." The answer might well come back from the Judge of all: "Interesting, but irrelevant." It is entirely possible that the universal God has his own question: "What I really want to know is how much of a human being with the spirit of Christ have you been as measured by your attitudes and actions toward other human beings?"

[9] *Ibid.*

76

"He is our peace." Is he? He "has broken down the dividing wall of hostility." Has he? He longs to help us, for he is the One who doesn't like a wall between his children. *He wants it down.*

PRAYER: O God, who hast made of one blood all nations of men for to dwell on the face of the earth, and didst send thy blessed Son Jesus Christ to preach peace to them that are nigh; discomfort us if we would twist the personality of others by our own false need to feel superior. Strengthen in us every impulse to love others as Christ loved, that in our own time despite any seeming differences we may live as neighbors with mutual respect and acceptance: one in him as we are one in thy sight. Amen.

Reveal the treasures of wisdom and knowledge
hidden in Christ, O God. Give us grace to un-
derstand and obey. For thy love's sake. Amen.

YOUR RIGHT TO DIFFER

SCRIPTURE: "We are no longer to be children, tossed by the waves and whirled about by every fresh gust of teaching, dupes of crafty rogues and their deceitful schemes. No, let us speak the truth in love; so shall we fully grow up into Christ" (Ephesians 4:14-15, *The New English Bible*).

Our theme is the right to differ. As our scriptural basis is in two verses of the Letter to the Ephesians, it may help briefly to comment on this remarkable epistle. Many persons consider it to be the greatest single piece of writing attributed to the apostle Paul. If it is not the greatest, it certainly ranks second only to the Letter to the Romans. Among famous Christians who have regarded it as outstanding were the famous reformer John Calvin, and the nineteenth-century English writer Samuel Taylor Coleridge. This letter is not always easy to follow. The difficulty may be due to our minds' inability to fly high enough to reach the altitude where Paul's mind soars. Notwithstanding certain biblical scholars' opinions to the contrary, we shall not go far wrong if we think of this letter as being written by Paul in prison in Rome near the end of his ministry. If it was written by a student-friend of Paul, as some believe, at least he expressed the great apostle's ideas, as Plato did those of Socrates. In this letter Paul is opening his mind to all the churches in the Ephesian mission field on the great theme of Christ and his church. "Here is none of the heat of controversy but rather a deep devotional spirit, as if the apostle himself were awed by the sublimities about which he was writing." [1]

Ephesians seems to fall into two main sections, the theological and practical. Rightly, the apostle linked faith and action. These are two sides of the same coin.

[1] William Neil, *Harper's Bible Commentary* (New York: Harper & Row, Publishers, 1963), p. 474.

I ask you to look at one of the practical implications of being a Christian as stressed by Paul. It is the role of the church in the world. This is the thrust of his argument: Christians must set an example of humility, patience, tolerance, and charity. God has ordained that Christians be one great fellowship; let us therefore strengthen our unity by fostering peace among ourselves. Let us never forget that the church is one, and not many, sustained by the same Spirit of God. Of course, each of us within the church has a separate function. The church should grow and mature, until it expresses the wholeness of Christ in its life.

The letter includes this observation: "We are no longer to be children, tossed by the waves and whirled about by every fresh gust of teaching, dupes of crafty rogues and their deceitful schemes" (Ephesians 4:14, *New English Bible*). We are to be mature enough not to be stampeded into conformity to something which we are convinced is not true, or not wise, or not Christian. Continues the apostle: "No, let us speak the truth [true belief and conduct as well as true speech] in love; so shall we fully grow up into Christ" (Ephesians 4:15, *The New English Bible*).

This is one significant expression of your right to differ from your fellow man and from your fellow Christian.

True, the right to differ on all issues confronting us *is a principle of a free society*. Among our cherished freedoms in our kind of national community is not only freedom of speech and of discussion but freedom to differ, sometimes sharply, sometimes even unfairly, with others. During the election campaign of former British Prime Minister Sir Alec Douglas-Home, a newsmagazine reported: "When heckling stirred an uproar in the crowd the Prime Minister was addressing at Aberfeldy, the Prime Minister calmly sat down in mid-speech, refusing to let party stewards throw out the interrupters. Said he, 'They are harmless people.'" [2]

One other conflict of opinion involved Chief Justice Warren of the United States Supreme Court. As our newspapers and magazines have pointed out, a great many Americans have been aggrieved at the actions of the Supreme Court under Mr. Justice Warren's leadership. The Court's civil rights decision has been anathema to Southern segregationists, many of whom in fact

[2] Reported in *Time* (Nov. 8, 1963), p. 38.

have demanded the Chief Justice's impeachment. Mr. Justice Warren is aware of the dissension, and at the 175th anniversary of Washington's Georgetown University he appealed for national unity. He cited the spirit of unity and reconciliation that prevailed when Chief Justice White, a Confederate Army veteran, and Oliver Wendell Holmes, a Union Army veteran, sat on the same bench as friends, and he pointed out that we need the same spirit as much now as we did then. Shortly after this appeal, Mr. Justice Warren went to New York to accept an honorary membership in the New York Bar Association. When he arrived, he found a band of jeering Birchist pickets waiting to heave placards at him. Said Warren: "It is a great thing that they can do this in this country."

Would you not agree that in our society — in the church, the university, and the legislatures — it is wisdom to prize criticism and differences of opinion as essentials to a healthy community? Every university administrator, president, or dean knows that the right to differ is essential to maintain academic freedom. The right of every faculty member to criticize and to differ from the majority has to be defended, even when the administrator himself disagrees with the professor's views. In any democratic community there must be freedom to differ as long as there is no incitement to violence. Our Lord said of evil and good, of error and truth: "Let both grow together until the harvest" (Matthew 13:30). Have we not seen, a dozen times over in the last half century, how men can lose their freedom either by overthrow from without their own country or by betrayal of the spirit of freedom within? Can anyone question the simple reasoning that Communism would soon put an end to what we know as a free society? This has been demonstrated many times; and Communism will do so again if and where it can. We must also recognize that the fear of Communism can betray us into snap judgments which may lead us to carry out grave injustices. Like many of you, I tend to grow impatient with some critics of our way of life in America. But I know that my impatience must never lead me to generalize blindly so that I equate criticism with treason. Writing some years ago, one of our noblest jurists, the late Justice Learned Hand, observed:

"What then is the spirit of liberty? I cannot define it; I can only tell you my own faith. The spirit of liberty is the spirit which

81

is not too sure that it is right; the spirit of liberty is the spirit which seeks to understand the minds of other men and women; the spirit of liberty is the spirit which weighs their interests alongside its own without bias; the spirit of liberty remembers that not even a sparrow falls to earth unheeded; the spirit of liberty is the spirit of Him who, near two thousand years ago, taught mankind that lesson it has never learned, but has never quite forgotten; that there may be a kingdom where the least shall be heard and considered side by side with the greatest." [3]

Judge Hand knew that the right to differ, the freedom to discuss and debate, derives from our spiritual heritage. Indeed, it is through the Hebrew-Christian faith in God and his purpose, in its doctrine of man and society that we find this right defended and declared. Actually to have to stress the right to differ is a footnote to one of history's so-called strange reversals, for in times past this right was taken for granted. Our climate today is much more favorable to conformity, to at least outwardly agreeing, than to diversity and individuality. But to those who would force us and others into certain precise patterns the Christian gospel has an unequivocal answer. Paul wrote, "Don't let the world around you squeeze you into its own mold, but let God remold your minds from within, so that you may prove in practice that the plan of God for you is good, meets all his demands and moves toward the goal of true maturity" (Romans 12:2, Phillips). Isn't this a scriptural way of saying, "Be yourself, honestly, even if you must dissent from others; even if you are a nonconformist"? God has made us as individuals. Infinite variety is everywhere in the design of life. Rollo May, psychologist, tells of two little girls who were twins. They were not only sisters but friends! Like many very small girls they wore matching dresses and outfits. When they were about three and a half years old the extroverted girl insisted on dressing differently from her sister. The wearing of identical dresses distressed her, and this fact puzzled her parents. They sought to learn why. Once they asked the little girl if when they went walking she did not like to have people on the street say, "Look at those nice twins." The little girl said vigorously, "No! I want them to say, 'Look at these two different people.'" That little girl ex-

[3] Learned Hand, *The Spirit of Liberty: Papers and Addresses of Learned Hand,* Irving Dilliard, ed. (New York: Alfred A. Knopf, Inc., 1960), p. 190.

pressed every person's need: to become a person in his own right. That need is, as Paul stated, "to prove in practice that God's plan for you is good, meets all his demands and moves toward the goal of true maturity."

To return to your right to differ from others, we now must remind ourselves that *when we do differ, when we do try to speak the truth as we see it but as others do not, there is one essential requirement laid upon us. We must "speak the truth in love."* Said John Baillie: "Love without truth won't do it, and neither will truth without love. Truth provides the light and love provides the heat, and both are needed for any healthy development into Christian manhood."[4] We may dislike the person's views and oppose them, but we have no right to be hostile to the person. Granted, it is not easy. This is why God gives us his grace. Christians may hate things, views, and conditions, but Christians may not hate people. Sometimes it is extremely hard not to hate people. I confess to you that the intelligent, hard-hitting nonconformist who is generally against everything that has been operating for even a few years, let alone those things that are fairly ancient in usage, tries my patience. I remember that I probably try his when I see value in some traditional matters, and I am not always convinced that what is new is true or desirable. In the Session of a Scottish kirk one elder whom we shall call Hamish MacGillicuddy opposed almost every innovation. When the elders decided to whitewash the church fence, he opposed spending the money and the whole idea in principle and in every other way. The other Session members voted for it. Pleaded the patient but harassed minister, "Hamish, on this fairly inconsequential question will you not make it unanimous?" "Never!" said the incorrigible nonconformist. "As long as I am a member of this kirk, nothing will be done unanimously!"

To those who even sharply differ with us, and with whom we differ, we must differ in love. We need not acquiesce; we may often need to give further interpretation. You know that it is sometimes said: "I disapprove of what you say, but I will defend to the death your right to say it." Can Christians do less? In our time, in our church, in our nation, there are sharp differences of opinion as to when, how, where, and to whom civil

[4] John Baillie, *A Reasoned Faith* (New York: Charles Scribner's Sons, 1963), p. 52.

rights shall be granted. Among Christians, as I have no doubt also among our Jewish brethren, there are differences of opinion as to how much church leaders, both lay and clerical, should participate in witnessing on behalf of equal rights and equal opportunities. We may differ and we must, but we must respect the right of others to their opinions. We may strive, as I think we have an obligation to do, to change them if we believe their opinions to be incorrect, but we must not do so by coercion. George Fox the Quaker and Oliver Cromwell the Puritan differed greatly about religion. One day they met and talked about "the perennials." When Fox rose to go, Cromwell said, "If thou and I were but one hour a day together, we should be nearer to the other. I wish no more harm to thee than to my own soul." That is the spirit to nourish. "We are no longer to be children, tossed by the waves and whirled about by every fresh gust of teaching [or emotion]. . . . No, let us speak the truth in love; so shall we fully grow up into Christ." An ancient motto expresses this truth: "In things essential, unity; in things doubtful, liberty; in all things, charity."

We must say one further thing: To maintain our right to differ, to insist that the follower of Christ must differ in love, does not mean that we can defer indefinitely the reaching of a decision. *We have a duty to decide.* If you are a scientist, teacher, parent, or counselor, you know that there is a time and a place for detachment and objectivity in life. But there is also a time and a place for devotion and commitment, and this the wiser ones know. Is there any single and significant relationship in life that can grow to its full meaning and stature without real commitment and dedication on the part of its participants?

We speak the truth in love in order that we and others may come to know and accept the truth. We have the right to differ without being labeled as reactionary, or rebellious, or perversely "agin'" the government, or a poor kind of Christian, or, on the racial question, a hater of our fellowmen whose skins are not the same color as ours. I am a little disturbed to hear that some respected educators were reported as saying that persons who are opposed to racially balanced schools are irrational. Some may be, but we cannot make such a general indictment of an opponent just because he disagrees with us. But we have a duty also to decide where we ourselves will stand. We can be detached, objective, and uncommitted about many things, but not about the great issues of justice versus injustice, freedom versus tyranny, truth versus falsehood, and kindness versus cruelty.

A world in which anything goes is a world in which everything goes. There is a time and a place for investigation, research, and conversation about such issues as civil rights, social freedoms, housing for minority group members, employment, and job training. But there is also a time to make up our minds. Protestant, Jewish, Eastern Orthodox, and Roman Catholic brethren are one in affirming that God calls us to work for a society in which all citizens have the rights and responsibilities which the nation's constitution declares belong to us all. As Christians we are also committed to speak and act so that all churches welcome worshipers regardless of their race, color, economic or social status. *You have the right to differ; you have the Christian duty to differ in love; you have the duty to decide for the right as God gives you to see the right.*

PRAYER: O God, who hast taught us that all our doings without love are worth nothing, forgive us what is lacking in our fellowship . . . for the barriers we have put up between one another, our lack of sensitiveness to one another's needs, discourtesy toward those who disagree with us, and our failure to help and encourage one another. Set us on the right path; grant that we discern thee in the issues of our time; and do thou perfect our fellowship in thee, by sending to us the Holy Spirit, through Jesus Christ in whose service there is perfect freedom. Amen.

*Let thy truth now be spoken in love and re-
ceived gladly that we see in it thyself; in Christ
our Lord. Amen.*

COPING WITH YOUR DISCONTENT

SCRIPTURE: "I rejoice in the Lord greatly that now at length you
have revived your concern for me; you were indeed concerned
for me, but you had no opportunity. Not that I complain of want;
for I have learned, in whatever state I am, to be content. I know
how to be abased, and I know how to abound; in any and all
circumstances I have learned the secret of facing plenty and
hunger, abundance and want. I can do all things in him who
strengthens me" (Philippians 4:10-13). "I have learned to find
resources in myself whatever my circumstances. I know what it
is to be brought low, and I know what it is to have plenty. I
have been very thoroughly initiated into the human lot with
all its ups and downs — fullness and hunger, plenty and want.
I have strength for anything through him who gives me power"
(Philippians 4:11-13, *New English Bible*). "I can do all things
through Him who infuses strength into me" (Philippians 4:13,
trans. by William Barclay).

Russell Baker, a newspaper columnist in Washington, D.C.,
told of a man's discontent with the imperious demands of a busy
telephone. This citizen went berserk in his home; he wrecked
his new Christmas phonograph and four record albums, and was
visited by the police after using regrettable language over the
telephone to a teen-ager. For ten days, the story goes, he had
been trying to settle down to listen without interruption to all
four records of *Tristan und Isolde* given him for Christmas. In
thirty-seven starts he never got beyond the overture without
having to answer the telephone. During his thirty-eighth attempt, he heard the overture to the end, only to be called to
the phone by his daughter's friend, Carol. She had called seven
times that day to ask if his daughter was at home yet. During
her six previous calls, he was interrupted at lunch, during a nap,
while watching a golf match on television, while reading a news-

paper, while reading the novel *Herzog*, and while trying to clean the rain gutters. On the seventh call, Mr. Baker discloses, the man's mind must have snapped and he unburdened himself to the teen-age caller. She said later that his language was absolutely vile. Then (I hope the story is considerably exaggerated) he proceeded to smash the hi-fi and the records, and was looking for a hatchet to put to the telephone when the representatives of law and order arrived!

The harassed man was unable to cope with one of the great conveniences and labor-saving devices of the twentieth century, the telephone. There are sound reasons for having a telephone. Nevertheless, our distraught friend objected to the fact that, like Pavlov's dogs which were conditioned to react to the ringing of a bell that symbolized food, most of us have been conditioned since childhood to stop everything and answer the telephone when it rings.

From so-called minor irritations to major ones, human beings find it difficult to cope with causes of their discontent. More than one man and woman have known what it means to try to live through the winter of discontent with their jobs or their achievement in their particular positions. Much unhappiness is experienced when human beings find that their married partners and the cares of the family make them unhappy, through frustration, deadly routine, and unrelieved or unshared responsibilities. It is not uncommon to know persons who are discontented with life as they have experienced it. Here is a person who is discontented because she is not married. There is another who is discontented because she is married. At a deeper level there are persons who could cope with life much more adequately if they could see any meaning in life.

How can you and I find resources to cope with our discontent? To cope means to fight or contend with, successfully or on equal terms. Christian faith should enable a man or woman to cope with whatever causes discontentment, inner frustration, or unhappiness. Indeed, can a Christian cope with the larger problems of life in community — poverty, discrimination, war, a city's renewal — unless he himself has peace at the center of his personality?

The New Testament shows us a Christian who found the secret of coping with life's ups and downs, disappointments and successes, failures and victories. The man is the apostle Paul. He writes of his secret in the letter we know as the Epistle to the Philippians. In contrast to other letters, Philippians is warmly affectionate, chatty, unsystematic, and directly concerned with the everyday living of members of a local congregation. Yet this letter contains some of Paul's finest insights. The contemporary biblical scholar Dr. William Neil says that this Philippian letter "is perhaps the best example of how some trifling issue in the life of a little Christian community sparks off in St. Paul's mind the kind of profound reflection which makes him the most creative thinker in the early Church." [1] This letter holds added interest when we learn that it was probably the apostle's swan song, written from prison. As his letter draws to a close, Paul tells his fellow Christians in Philippi how grateful he is for the gift of money they have sent him. To him it has meant much that they cared for him and showed it in such a practical fashion. Then he assures them that he has not been dissatisfied with his own condition. He has learned the art of contentment. "I have learned to find resources in myself whatever my circumstances. I know what it is to be brought low, and I know what it is to have plenty. I have been very thoroughly initiated into the human lot with all its ups and downs — fullness and hunger, plenty and want."

What does this tell us who live in the present-day world about how to cope with our ups and downs, particularly the "downs"? The secret seems to be twofold. One part of it is psychological. The other part is theological, or spiritual.

We learn to cope with our discontent *when we learn to find resources in ourselves whatever our circumstances.* This means surely that, from time to time, we learn the necessity of detaching ourselves from our schedules, our duties, and our crowded calendars. Paul himself went into Arabia to sort out his values, to gain a truer perspective of his life and work. Jesus our Lord went into a desert place, into a quiet retreat with his disciples, not for permanent escape from the world but that he might renew his physical and spiritual strength in order to return to the world better able to cope with the world's demands and needs. I recall the wise counsel given me when I was installed in an early pastorate. It was given by an experienced older pastor. In his charge

[1] Neil, *op. cit.,* p. 478.

to the pastor-elect he said, "Be sure to take your day off every week. If anyone criticizes you and says the devil takes no time off from his work, you tell him that this is one of the reasons why he is a devil!"

Detachment may be made in other ways than by a vacation from work and the daily round. In such times it is good to gain a truer perspective on that which makes us discontented with our own achievement. We may learn that if we have not won as many of the glittering prizes of success as we once thought we would, we may have contributed something worthwhile through our work. We cannot measure our achievement by the amount of money we may have received or saved. In most cases accomplishment and financial return bear little relationship to each other. It is possible that a man may have great achievements and very little pay or, conversely, that he may have colossal pay or salary and very few real achievements. John Milton received for the manuscript of his monumental poem *Paradise Lost* exactly ninety dollars. A few years ago two American pugilists pummeled each other for some twenty minutes and divided a purse of two million dollars. Are we to conclude that these prize fighters were twenty thousand times more successful than John Milton? Again, when we take time out to reflect, we may realize that many of our significant contributions have escaped our notice completely. When Mozart died in abject poverty at the age of thirty-five, his achievements in music must have seemed small, even to those who knew him best. But whenever Mozart's music is played today we are able to recognize it as truly great creative work. Even if we do not have a success in the world's view, we may nevertheless be successful in terms of becoming a real person.

When Paul wrote "I have learned, in whatever state I am, to be content," the word translated "content" was borrowed from Stoic philosophy. Literally it means "entirely self-sufficient" or "independent." It was a maxim of the Stoic philosophers that a man's real life was in his own soul, that he might not depend on outward circumstances or good or bad breaks, but should be sufficient to himself. Paul says that his life-experience taught him this lesson, although it was through a discipline different from that practiced by the Stoics. He has had a troubled life, but now he is able to put up with whatever comes and be inwardly content. Then he turns to the mystery religions of his time and

90

borrows another word translated in the Revised Standard Version "*I have learned the secret* of facing plenty and hunger, abundance and want." "I have learned the secret" is literally, "I have been thoroughly initiated" — that is, admitted to the inner secrets. God offers every one of his children a chance to develop his latent powers, to build a dependable, fine character, and to perform faithfully and well at least one job his community needs if it is to move forward socially and morally as scientific and external progress takes place. Each one can throw the so-called stubborn ounces of his weight behind some cause devoted to making this a better world. To help support the fabric of a decent world is no small matter. However obscure, however unpublicized your life may be, you *are* a success. What did the Master of the Art of Living say? "A man's life consisteth not in the abundance of the things which he possesseth" (Luke 12:15, King James Version). "For a man's real life in no way depends upon the number of his possessions" (Luke 12:15, Phillips). Do you remember Christ's definition of achievement? "Whoever would be first among you must be slave of all" (Mark 10:44).

Is this all we learn from Paul about coping with our discontent? No, and if the psychological insights were all that Paul had to give, they would have been superseded long ago. Indeed, Paul would not be read and studied if he had been only a wise teacher of philosophy. For all their noble discipline and attainments, the Stoics "made of the heart a desert, and called it a peace." The Stoic of the ancient world, like the person who is stoical today, resolves to be content with whatever is and whatever happens by deliberate act of will. Paul knows how undependable the will alone can be. *So Paul gives us the heart of the secret of coping with discontent. It is in verse 13 of this fourth chapter of Philippians: "I can do all things through Christ which strengtheneth me"* (King James Version). I like the translation: "I am ready for anything through the strength of the one who lives within me" (Phillips). Professor William Barclay is sure Paul wrote, "I can do all things through Christ who *infuses* His strength into me." The verb "strengthens" means "infuses power into." You say this is a kind of Christ-mysticism that is beyond you? Is it? To be with Christ, to be a living member of Christ's body or company, is to be "in Christ" and to have his spirit, his grace, and his power within. In this changing world, with its crosses and crises and its ups and downs, you and I do not need to go to pieces — to be up one day and down the next. Some people come apart at the seams because they have too little; some have been shattered because they have had too much. This is why Jesus saw trouble ahead for some very rich people, and why he said it is hard for a rich man to enter the kingdom of heaven. Many of us need to be much more discontented than we are with things around us. But many of us also need to know the tremendous secret of keeping life on an even keel by the power of a great stabilizer. Oliver Cromwell's name is one linked with this secret. When he was critically ill, as well as saddened by the death of his wife, he called for his Bible. After he asked that one of those present read the passage from the fourth chapter of Philippians, Cromwell is said to have testified: "This Scripture did once save my life, when my eldest son died; which went as a dagger to my heart; indeed it did." Cromwell then repeated the words of the text and commented, "It is true, Paul, *you* have learned this, and attained to this measure of grace; but what shall I do? Ah, poor creature, it is a hard lesson for me to take out! I find it so!" Then he read Paul's statement: *"I can do all things through Christ that strengtheneth me."* As faith began to work, his heart was strengthened, and he said to himself, "He that was Paul's Christ is my Christ too!"

To face each day, each problem, each opportunity, each task with Christ and in Christ, is the secret. Walk with Christ, live *in* Christ, and you can cope with anything.

PRAYER: Loving Father, in whose will is our peace and in whose service is perfect freedom, set us free from all unworthy discontent. In the midst of our spiritual warfare for Christ's cause grant us peace at the center of our lives. So may we serve thee with quiet and contented minds even while we oppose all that is contrary to thy will. For thy love's sake we ask it. Amen.

*Let our ears and minds and hearts be open to
thy word for us now: in Jesus Christ the living
Word. Amen.*

CHRISTIAN MANNERS
IN TIMES OF STRESS

SCRIPTURE: "Love is patient and kind; love is not jealous, or conceited, or proud; love is not ill-mannered, or selfish, or irritable; love does not keep a record of wrongs; love is not happy with evil, but is happy with the truth. Love never gives up: its faith, hope, and patience never fail" (1 Corinthians 13:4-7, *Today's English Version*). "Next, as regards brotherly love, you don't need any written instructions. God himself is teaching you to love one another. . . . Yet we urge you to have more and more of this love" (1 Thessalonians 4:9, 10, Phillips).

On the stone mantelpiece of a fireplace in a meeting room in a Protestant church in Montreal, three words were carved. They were written in the fourteenth century by a man who was both a bishop and a chancellor of England. He is known as William of Wykeham, the man who founded two colleges (Winchester College and New College, Oxford). Here are the three words: *"Manners maketh man."*

Do they? Granted, when manners are defined as forms of politeness they make life more pleasant, but do they contribute to the making of a man or woman? In times of stress are they not obsolete, or at least superfluous? When a house is burning, no one approaches a fireman or policeman, raises his hat, introduces himself, and then asks politely, "Excuse me but could someone try to rescue a man in one of the rooms in the house? I think someone has been overcome by smoke. Thank you very much." Accordingly, it is argued that when the health and well-being of persons, or of an entire community are at stake, there is no time for what we call manners or good manners. For long enough, the argument goes, people who have tried to reform evil conditions have been polite, correct, and persistent, while not much improvement seems to have happened. When we are rough and tough we get attention and action, and the rough and tough leaders demonstrate to cynical and skeptical followers that they mean business and can be trusted. You and I may have some sympathy for this position, and see some reasoning in this defense of the abrasive language, the rough and rude approach which provokes response.

Nevertheless, there is one consideration which too often seems to be overlooked or written off. It is this: A Christian is a person who follows Jesus Christ. True, Jesus Christ spoke harshly of groups of persons in the Palestinian society of his time. He was not always meek and gentle in the modern meaning of these terms. Notwithstanding, Jesus Christ was, as David Livingstone said, the most perfect gentleman. Christ was impeccably courteous to such people as a prostitute (the woman taken in adultery), a grafter (Zaccheus), and a hardened criminal undergoing execution (the thief on the cross beside him at Calvary).

Jesus our Lord taught the ethics of love. This love was not what a youngster might call a soupy thing. The love of God which animated Christ was strong and discerning, but on the other hand it was unfailingly kind. Here is a famous description of this love:

". . . Love is patient and kind; love is not jealous, or conceited, or proud; *Love is not ill-mannered* [italics ours], or selfish, or irritable; love does not keep a record of wrongs; love is not happy with evil, but is happy with the truth. Love never gives up: its faith, hope, and patience never fail" (1 Corinthians 13: 4-7, *Today's English Version*).

What is a Christian? A Christian is a person who has changed his mind so that he turns from being in orbit around himself to being in orbit around God in Christ (the old word is "repented"); he has confided himself to Christ, has put his whole trust in Christ, and has pledged his life to be a follower and servant of Christ for life.

What does it mean to live as a Christian? It means many things. I like the suggestion that we can understand the meaning of a Christian life by the use of three prepositions. It is life *after* Christ, it is life *in* Christ, and it is life *for* Christ. The apostle Paul describes the Christian life as *kata Christon,* that is, life after the manner of Christ, according to the character and example of Christ. Paul said "May God . . . grant that you may

94

agree with one another *after the manner of Christ Jesus . . .*" (Romans 15:5, *New English Bible*, italics ours). Christ's life is a pattern or example which we are to follow. In the Gospels and in the letters of the New Testament we see this pattern clearly. The apostle writes, "Therefore be imitators of God, as beloved children. And walk in love, as Christ loved us and gave himself up for us . . ." (Ephesians 5:1-2). "Try to be like him, and live in love as Christ loved you" (Ephesians 5:1-2, *New English Bible*). The apostle Peter also refers to the suffering and sacrifice of Christ when he speaks of Christ as our pattern: "For to this you have been called, because Christ also suffered for you, leaving you an example, that you should follow in his steps" (1 Peter 2:21).

Would anyone say that this example which we have in Christ is one of arrogance, of aggressiveness, of rudeness? Who could believe such a thing, once he has read of the conduct, the spirit, and the grace of this Man? Throughout the centuries, beginning with the first of the Christian era, men and women who knew him — and know him — spoke of his patience, gentleness, magnanimity, forgiveness, humility, service, and graciousness. Says the writer of the first letter of John, "Whoever claims to be dwelling in him, binds himself to live *as Christ himself lived*" (1 John 2:6, *New English Bible*, italics ours).

Granted, this is a huge order. It is admitted, too, that most of us fail "to live as Christ himself lived." To be a Christian is to live according to Christ's character and example. To be a Christian is to live *after* Christ. This means that we are to follow after him; to imitate him. This would be hopelessly discouraging and impossible, were it not that we are to live *in* Christ. If Christ were no more than our perfect example, we would turn away utterly despairing of ever becoming Christian. But Christ is not outside and separate from Christians. We are *united* with Christ in trusting faith, through our baptism, through our commitment to him, through our membership in his body, the church, the community. This phrase "in Christ" is used 164 times in Paul's letters. We can understand something of what it means when we think of Jesus' allegory of the vine and the branches. In the Old Testament the vine was a symbol of Israel, God's people. In the New Testament Christ is the true Israel. He is the vine, and his followers are the branches. Life in Christ is life together with the people of God. Christians are together, like fingers of the hand. As birds fly *in* the air, as fish swim *in* the sea, as plants grow *in* the soil, so Christians are together *in* Christ. Being together in the vine, we derive life from it, and nourishment, and then as branches we bring forth fruit. Then our life is *for* Christ.

What are the practical effects of this truth? Surely this, that drawing strength from the vine, drawing grace from Christ, we are to be like him toward our brothers and sisters in the Christian fellowship. Dietrich Bonhoeffer has a clear word for us here, in his luminous little book *Life Together:* "When God was merciful to us, we learned to be merciful with our brethren. When we received forgiveness instead of judgment, we, too, were made ready to forgive our brethren. What God did to us, we then owed to others. . . . Thus God Himself taught us to meet one another as God has met us in Christ." [1] "Welcome one another, therefore, as Christ has welcomed you, for the glory of God" (Romans 15:7).

To follow Christ in his style of living, to imitate Christ as we are given divine power or grace to imitate him, means surely that we show love not only to the brethren, those who are members of the Christian community — but that this love is never ill-mannered or rude to any of God's children.

Surely, *it means that we treat even our opponents as persons who may be misguided, who may be wrong, but persons deserving the benefit of the doubt.* It surely means that, instead of a quick victory which only hardens the opposition, *we seek reconciliation.* Are not Christians to act and speak above the average and ahead of nonchristians? Are we not engaged in the ministry of reconciliation? Do we reconcile another by blasting him? Is it not possible that we are not always completely right? I like those words of Oliver Cromwell to the Westminster Assembly of the Divines, who like some Presbyterians in every age, were convinced they were absolutely, unequivocally right in their position. Said Cromwell to them, "I beseech you, by the mercies of Christ, to consider that you may be mistaken!"

Christlike love is very patient and very kind; it is never rude. It is never happy when others go wrong. It is happy in the

---

[1] Dietrich Bonhoeffer, *Life Together,* J. W. Doberstein, trans. (New York: Harper & Row, Publishers, 1954), pp. 24-25.

truth. "There is a graciousness in Christian love which never forgets that courtesy and tact and politeness may possibly be regarded as lesser virtues but they are lovely things."[2] It is not a sign of weakness, but of strength. You may recall the feud between Abraham Lincoln and Secretary of State Stanton. Stanton called Lincoln "a low, cunning clown," "the original gorilla." Lincoln said nothing. He made Stanton his Secretary of War because he considered him to be the best for the job. He treated Stanton with every courtesy. The years went on. The night came when the assassin's bullet murdered Lincoln in the theater. In the little room where he lay, the same Stanton looked down through his tears and said, "There lies the greatest ruler the world has ever seen."[3]

What does it mean in ways we can practice? *This: That we listen to others and speak with others, as we believe Christ would want us to listen and speak.* This means that we cannot hate a person or a group of persons. We may hate evil but never the evildoer. Listen to the Scripture: "Do not speak evil against one another, brethren. He that speaks evil against a brother or judges his brother, speaks evil against the law and judges the law. But if you judge the law, you are not a doer of the law but a judge. There is one lawgiver and judge, he who is able to save and to destroy. But who are you that you judge your neighbor?" (James 4:11-12). This verse is quoted by Bonhoeffer in his discussion of ministry in *Life Together*.

During a recent controversy, a highly respected Christian layman who represented one side of the argument wrote me that what appalled him more than being accused of being wrong in policy and action was the personal abuse he received from Christian ministers. I, too, was appalled. Naturally I apologized for my brothers. I recalled the clear rebuke of the apostle where he begged the Ephesian Christians *to live a life worthy of their calling,* "with humility and patience, making allowances for one another because you love one another. Make it your aim to be at one in the Spirit, and you will inevitably be at peace with one another" (Ephesians 4:2-3, Phillips). "Give up living like

[2] William Barclay, *The Letters to the Corinthians* in *The Daily Study Bible Series* (Edinburgh: The Saint Andrew Press, 1956; and Philadelphia: The Westminster Press, 1958), p. 133.
[3] *Ibid.*

pagans. . . . That is not how you learned Christ" (Ephesians 4:17, 20, *The New English Bible*). "Christian manners" means being sensitive to the needs of others, whoever they may be.

How do we "learn Christ"? How do we attain the love that seeks not her own, that is kind, patient, courteous? Only with Christ, and in Christ. *Over his life, and over his Cross could be written: "Love is patient and kind . . . love is not ill-mannered, or selfish . . . love does not keep a record of wrongs; love is not happy with evil. . . . Love never gives up."* A scholar and college administrator, the late Principal Rainey was noted for his gracious manners, even under stress. Colleagues joked about his habitual response when he was walking with another person. He always said, "You first, I follow." When this good servant of Christ was slipping away from this life, those near his bed heard him whisper as to another he had served many years, "You first, I follow."

PRAYER: Lord, we love thee but not enough. We follow Christ, but not really as we should. Fill us with thy love that we love in attitude and action, in speech and silence. Amen.

Let the voice of Christ speak to us through the words of Scripture and through thy servant. For thy love's sake. Amen.

THE HARDEST QUESTION HUMANS ASK

SCRIPTURE: "And the servants of the householder came and said to him, 'Sir, did you not sow good seed in your field? How then has it weeds?' He said to them, 'An enemy has done this'" (Matthew 13:27-28). "Now is the judgment of this world, now shall the ruler of this world be cast out; and I, when I am lifted up from the earth, will draw all men to myself" (John 12:31-32).

What is the hardest question human beings ask? It is the question: "Why do people suffer?" When this question is asked, the questioner obviously means, "Why do good people suffer?" It is wholesome to ask this question, and to ask it not in the hushed tones which are often used in a funeral home. It is good to try to find an answer, however tentative, however inadequate, when the sun of health and well-being is shining, and not when sorrow strikes, or pain lacerates body and mind.

One answer which commends itself to a Christian believer — to one who trusts that at the heart of all existence and around, beyond, and within us is holy, righteous, compassionate Love — is found in the words of the householder in Jesus' parable of the wheat and the tares. Hear now the story told by Jesus in *Today's English Version:*

"Jesus told them another parable: 'The Kingdom of heaven is like a man who sowed good seed in his field. One night, when everyone was asleep, an enemy came and sowed weeds among the wheat, and went away. When the plants grew and the heads of grain began to form, then the weeds showed up. The man's servants came to him and said, "Sir, it was good seed you sowed in your field; where did the weeds come from?" "It was some enemy who did this," he answered'" (Matthew 13:24-28).

Unmerited suffering is here. Pain is one of life's realities. To live is to suffer at times. Jesus accepted this as a fact. "In the world [in your life] you have tribulation" (John 16:33). Paul

99

said we should take our share of hardship. Hardship, suffering, and pain are realities of life on this planet. One man put it this way:

"One day cancer strikes; one day a plane crashes; one day a foot slips off a ladder; one day a child opens a medicine bottle; one day a father gasps in the sudden pain of a heart attack; one day a mother dies and leaves a young family. . . . And through them all the same questions run: How and why and who? God? The devil? Chance? 'What shall we say to this?' cries Paul, facing as every age and every man faces, the same problem of human pain and suffering and the mystery of its origin and meaning. . . . Beyond the personal disasters and tragedies there are the impersonal. An earthquake shatters a city and hundreds, young and old, lie dead in the ruins; a volcano erupts and snuffs out with its hot breath a whole valley, man and beast and leaf; a tidal wave surges in silently from the sea and sweeps its helpless victims away; a hurricane slams into the coast and leaves a swath of destruction and death; an epidemic decimates a whole community, leaving tears and bitterness. . . . Why? How? Who? God? Evil? Fate? Nature? Is there any purpose of any meaning? Is there any comfort? What then shall we say to these things?" [1]

We must quickly acknowledge that there is no completely satisfactory explanation, no completely adequate solution to this age-old worldwide problem. As Christians we must say, "An enemy has done this." What enemy? Evil. Certainly not God, although he is frequently blamed for our suffering, our defeats, our pain. "What did I do that God would send this to me?" persons still ask in their agony. "Why did God do this to me? Why did God allow this to happen?" For the Christian, or for the Jewish believer in God, in fact for any religious person, the problem is more acute. Not only in our personal and family lives does suffering and trouble come; the world is full of it.

What shall we say to these things? This, at least: *God has not willed it*. It is really blasphemous to attribute suffering and pain to the God and Father of us all, the God and Father of Jesus Christ. In James Agee's novel *A Death in the Family*, the young husband is killed in a senseless one-car accident. A little bolt came loose and the car swerved off the highway. Later, when

[1] Hubert Black, *Good God! Cry or Credo* (Nashville: Abingdon Press, 1966), pp. 18, 19.

the young widow's brother came to be with her, "she felt that he was saying, 'And you can still believe in that idiot God of yours?' " [2] We are not to bow in supine resignation before unmerited, undeserved pain or bereavement and say "It is God's will." Suffering, pain, and death are not God's will. Jesus treated disease as demonic, an evil, and he cured persons of disease whenever he could. The Scriptures call death "the last enemy to be destroyed." It surely cannot be God's original purpose that man should suffer and die. Here let me commend the twentieth-century classic treatment of the will of God to any who have not read it. It is the book by Leslie D. Weatherhead entitled *The Will of God*. In it he writes of the "intentional will of God," "the circumstantial will of God," and "the Ultimate Will of God." God's original purpose is that man shall find his existence to be good, and without pain. In the Bible we are given the picture of God's ultimate purpose being realized when there shall be "a new heaven and a new earth . . . and death shall be no more, neither shall there be mourning nor crying nor pain any more" (Revelation 21:1, 4). We may suffer as we strive to do God's will in a given situation. But God does not send the suffering. If I give up some debilitating habit — say I am a drug addict — I will suffer withdrawal pains, but while God desires me to be whole and healed, and the process of becoming so entails suffering, God does not send the suffering. Leslie Weatherhead comments: "When we say . . . that nothing can happen unless it is God's will . . . we mean, [or should mean] that nothing can happen which can *finally* defeat him." [3] Death, we say, comes as a friend to some loved one who has suffered a cruel, lingering illness. But really, death is the lesser of two evils. Ask an older person and you would find that he would agree with Maurice Chevalier, who, when asked if he resented growing old, is said to have replied with his inimitable charm, "Not when you consider the alternative." Christians believe that God has conquered death, but it is not part of the Christian faith that physical death is good in itself. Death is the last enemy that God will overthrow. So we must be careful when we are tempted to say, "God has

[2] James Agee, *A Death in the Family* (New York: McDowell, Obelensky, Inc., 1956), p. 120.
[3] Leslie D. Weatherhead, *The Will of God* (New York: Abingdon Press, 1944), p. 33.

chosen you to suffer for his glory." *God is not a sadist.* Would a normal loving parent show his love by deliberately making his child deformed or retarded? What human parent would inflict suffering and say, "I am doing this for your own good, because I love you"? God, to be God, must be at least as good as the best father or mother. Jesus said, "If you then, who are evil, know how to give good gifts to your children, how much more will your Father who is in heaven give good things to those who ask him?" (Matthew 7:11).

Why do human beings suffer? "Because an enemy has done this." We need not think of the enemy as a stereotyped stage devil with horns, tail, and pitchfork, dressed in fiery red. God has given freedom, and man has abused it. Evil has come into the very order of things. Evil is present in us, along with the good. God asks us to use our freedom to join him in defeating the evil. Whether we do so or not, God will vanquish the evil at last.

But is not some suffering beneficial? Is not pain a source of ultimate good? I would prefer to say that the ways in which we make use of suffering may contain ultimate good. But in themselves, suffering, sin, and death are evils to be overthrown, to be fought.

Someone has classified suffering in two categories, *punitive* and *remedial.* Punitive suffering occurs not by God's action but by our own wrongdoing. If I smoke cigarettes excessively, I may punish myself by developing emphysema, lung cancer, or arterial trouble. Then God is not punishing me; I am suffering as a direct result of my own folly and self-indulgence. Between *some* suffering and sin there is a direct causal relationship. Our Lord was sure that whatever a man sows, that he also reaps. That which is reaped may be evil; it may be good. Guilt may be personal or corporate. We blamed General Short and Admiral Kimmel for the tragedy of Pearl Harbor in December, 1941, but we are now more disposed to distribute the blame among many, including the President, the State Department, the America First Committee, and our own illusion that it would never happen to us. Like sheep, we have all gone astray (see Isaiah 53:6).

Some suffering may be remedial or educative. We believe that there is no neat system of equal rewards and punishments in this human life of ours. We are to live in a dynamic relationship with God, and in that relationship God does help us to use suffering to reshape ourselves into mature, responsible members of God's family. Good parents do not always shield their children from a painful experience if it promises to be remedial. But the pain should have some purpose and not be out of proportion to the action. The Letter to the Hebrews said that even Jesus, the Son of God, learned by what he suffered. God did not send his Son to suffer or to die, but to save the world. The death of Jesus surely was not decreed by the loving Father. The idea that *an enemy has done this* is implied in the New Testament and our gospel.

This mention of the cross of Christ brings us to say that, although God never wills evil, God does give grace to those who suffer from their own folly, their wrong choices, or from the demonic forces in the world. Grace for what? *Grace to use the pain and the sorrow redemptively.* To find suffering redemptive, we must always volunteer for it. Each man, each woman, must take up the cross for himself or herself. "Cross-bearing is voluntary suffering for Christ's sake." [4] Jesus could have bypassed Calvary. So can you, and so can I. "No one takes my life away from me," said Jesus. He chose to do God's will, to be the pioneer of a new way for man.

Is this all we can say to anyone who is suffering? No, it is not. Unshared pain, unshared trouble, can destroy a person. Everyone needs a friend. When Edvard Grieg composed the musical setting for Henrik Ibsen's poem "Peer Gynt," he played it on the piano for Ibsen. When Ibsen heard it, he gripped Grieg's hand and whispered, "Understood! Understood!" When anyone turns to Christ in the loneliness of mental, spiritual, or physical pain, he knows that he is understood. Says the writer of the Letter to Hebrews:

"Let us, then, hold firmly to the faith we profess. For we have a great high priest who has gone into the very presence of God — Jesus, the Son of God. Our high priest is not one who cannot feel sympathy with our weaknesses. On the contrary, we have a high priest who was tempted in every way that we are, but did not sin. Let us be brave, then, and come forward to God's

---

[4] Wallace E. Fisher, *Preaching and Parish Renewal* (Nashville: Abingdon Press, 1966), p. 65.

throne, where there is grace. There we will receive mercy and find grace to help us just when we need it" (Hebrews 4:14-16, *Today's English Version*).

PRAYER: O Love Divine that stoops to share our sharpest pang, our bitterest tear, we praise thee that thou art a God of love and that thou art working to conquer pain and sin and death. We thank thee that thou art active also in promoting and encouraging all good. Help us to choose the good and thereby have thy energy working in us, and Christ living within and beside us. Send us out today and tomorrow with the confidence that thy love is invincible, and that in this love we can meet everything which comes to us. These favors we ask through Jesus Christ, thy Son, our Lord. Amen.

Fulfill now thy promise, that the entrance of thy Word may give us light and the coming of thy grace may give us love in Christ our Lord. Amen.

ENTER GOD—
WHEN ALL SEEMS TO BE AGAINST US

SCRIPTURE: "Jacob their father said unto them, Me have ye bereaved of my children: Joseph is not, and Simeon is not, and ye will take Benjamin away: all these things are against me" (Genesis 42:36, King James Version).

Do you sometimes feel as if you can't win? Are there too many adverse factors working in your situation for you to cope successfully with life? It is human to grow discouraged about one's own personality, his vocation, his chance of genuine love, his marriage, or his failure to marry. Moreover, in the arena of larger issues more than one citizen has felt that the persons and groups which are against a good cause are too strong.

Several years ago a cartoon showed two weird-looking characters parading along a city sidewalk. Each of them carried a sign. One was an elderly but unsmiling individual with long hair and beard. Inscribed on his sign were the words THE WORLD IS COMING TO AN END. He was closely followed by an equally pessimistic man whose sign read THANK HEAVEN![1]

In the Book of Genesis, Jacob is shown in such a mood. The father of Joseph and his brothers has been through a series of calamities. The last straw is laid on his pile of woe when his sons return from their attempt to get grain from the Egyptian government. Jacob learns that money has been planted in the luggage of his sons, and that his son Simeon is being held hostage by the lord of the land of Egypt until they return with the youngest son Benjamin. He is sure his world is coming to an end.

"Jacob their father said unto them, Me have ye bereaved of my children: Joseph is not, and Simeon is not, and ye will take Benjamin away: all these things are against me."

[1] The *New Yorker* magazine, February 22, 1964.

Strangers looking at most of us would not imagine that any of us experience moods like that of Jacob. We look like representatives of the most affluent society the earth has known. Casual onlookers would never guess that we might feel we are up against something that is too much for us, that at times we may even feel cheated of our rights or even persecuted. Yet, as Tennyson's saying goes, "Never morning wore to evening but some heart did break." If one's heart does not actually break, his heart — the spirit within — may sink to a new low. In the popular language of our day, yet in all seriousness, we are likely to say "I've been robbed. I've been robbed of someone I loved, of the chance I worked for, of health, of happiness." The more public-spirited of us who have supported great causes, such as racial justice and harmony, may feel we have been robbed of victory in our time by powerful forces which are determined to block the advance begun in recent years. Christians who have devoted time, energy, prayer, and money to the church are troubled by attacks on the community of Christ in its institutional forms, not only by enemies from without but by fierce critics within her fellowship. In addition, they note the widespread apathy concerning the church's mission in today's world.

In one relationship or another, whether in our intimate personal lives or in the areas of social concern, we could say with depressed Jacob of long ago:

"Me have ye bereaved of my children: Joseph is not, and Simeon is not, and ye will take Benjamin away: all these things are against me."

"Enter God" when everyone and everything seems to be against us. How does God enter into the situation when we feel outnumbered, outmaneuvered, beaten? God enters as he always does, in the power of his Spirit. God is involved in all that is. Even when we are completely unaware of his presence and activity, he is ceaselessly active. Wrote the apostle to the struggling young church in Philippi: "God is at work in you, both to will and to work for his good pleasure" (Philippians 2:13). An ancient prayer says:

"Almighty and eternal God, strengthen this thy servant, we beseech thee, with the Holy Spirit the Comforter, and daily increase in him thy manifold gifts of grace: the spirit of wisdom and understanding, the spirit of counsel and might, the spirit of knowledge and of the fear of the Lord; and keep him in thy mercy unto life eternal; through Jesus Christ our Lord."

Enter God, through "the spirit of wisdom and understanding, the spirit of counsel and might, the spirit of knowledge and of the fear of the Lord." This is true godliness. God is the infinite factor in our human situation, giving us a truer perspective than when we feel that everyone and everything is against us.

When we open our minds to the Spirit of wisdom and understanding, *we are likely to discover that some of our trouble comes not from external enemies or outside forces, but from within ourselves.* Jacob may have been led to self-discovery. It has been said that Jacob was a perfect picture of man in miniature. A true reading of Jacob would support Jeremiah's view: "The heart is deceitful above all things, and desperately corrupt" (Jeremiah 17:9). The name "Jacob" comes from a Hebrew word which has to do with a heel. This goes back to the circumstances of his birth. It is told that Esau, the elder of twins, was born with the hand of the younger Jacob holding his heel; that is, according to the story, even in the moment of birth Jacob was trying to hold his brother back and secure first place for himself! Thus he was called Jacob, "the one who takes by the heel" (or the one who tries to supplant). I have no idea whether the slang expression which describes a man as a "heel" can be traced back to Jacob! Probably we mean to say that since the heel of a human being is the lowest part of the body, a man who is a heel is the lowest of the low. Jacob tricked his brother out of his birthright. He deceived his own father. He tricked his uncle. Indeed, Jacob was such a crooked promoter that he made his father-in-law Laban happy when he announced that he was going back home. Laban's parting word was a prayer that is widely known as the Mizpah benediction, "The Lord watch between you and me, when we are absent one from the other." Originally this was not at all a pious prayer for God's blessing; it really meant, "May God keep his eye on you and me when we can't keep our eyes on each other!" Can this reading of Jacob also be true of ourselves?

When everyone and everything seems against us, we may need some searching self-scrutiny. "Woe to you when all men speak well of you," said Jesus (Luke 6:26). To be popular with everyone may mean that we stand for nothing that is worthwhile.

But it is also serious when no one speaks well of us. Lest we be unaware of our vulnerability, we may need to do some homework on the study of ourselves. Are we standing for the difficult right against the lazy wrong, or are we just cantankerous, mean, and miserable? Are we patient enough? Are we fair? Are we genuinely interested in others? Do we really love our neighbors with Christlike love so that we desire and seek their best? Are we a little kinder than necessary? If someone asks us to go one mile of service, are we cheerfully willing to go two miles for him? Or are we possessive? Do we try to play the part of God, and move persons around (always, of course, "for their own good," and not for our own profit)? Or do we look on others not from a human point of view, but with something of the insight of Christ?

When all things are against us, and God has shown us that almost invariably our own limitations, our own failures, and our own sins are contributing factors, what help then is there for us?

1. *God enters through the Spirit of his Son Jesus Christ to offer us a new life.* Jacob was a heel. He did not remain that way. He became God's helper. A man, even a heel, knows that he is made for something better than the dirt. Jacob the heel received a new name. He was called "Israel," which means "a prince of God." Jacob had a spiritual experience, mediated through his famous dream. Wrestling with an unknown traveler, Jacob realized that his real enemy was not Esau his brother, whom he had defrauded, but God himself. He discovered — as the forces of tyranny, falsehood, injustice, and inhumanity always discover sooner or later — that man cannot fight God. When Jacob told his mysterious wrestling opponent at the brook Jabbok that his name was Jacob, he was told: "Your name shall no more be called Jacob, but Israel, for you have striven with God and with men, and have prevailed" (Genesis 32:28). "Israel" means "prince" or "perseverer with God." God entered into Jacob's life transformingly. Jacob did not like the man he was and, through God's enabling power, he became a helper, a prince of a man.

2. The picture of Jacob bears a resemblance to ourselves. His story and that of countless others reminds us of the Salvation Army's phrase: "Saved to serve." Jacob was being fitted for a task. He was called by God, and was changed in the inward

man by the Spirit of God to be a servant. He gave his new name forever after to God's chosen people, not for privilege but for service. In the New Testament the church, the people of God, is described as the "new Israel." You and I are called to be Christians, servants of God and God's children. To be a servant in the Christian sense is to engage in Christianizing.

3. To be numbered among the servants of God and his children means that we are in the blessed company of faithful people, the living church. In such fellowship we know that many are *for us*. We are human, and because we are, we crave the companionship of a beloved community. Man was never made to stand alone. He needs the society of his brothers and sisters. He needs to be with others as he faces the ultimate mysteries of life, death, and eternity. You want the city of God. You need the church, however much you deny it.

When all these things are against us, and every man's hand seems to be raised against us to thwart us and defeat us, *God enters into our awareness to show us that the conclusion which seems to be so obvious can be false.* Jacob was sure that he had lost his sons. "Me have ye bereaved of my children: Joseph is not, and Simeon is not, and ye will take Benjamin away: all these things are against me." To Jacob it seemed obvious. But the obvious was not true. Jacob learned that the sons he thought he had lost were alive and doing extremely well. His own boy Joseph was the governor of all Egypt, and was the lord he had feared. Instead of all things in Jacob's life going wrong, the actual situation, when it became known to him, proved that the best was yet to be.

But I cannot leave you with Jacob, or Israel, for I would commend you to the care of One who was founder of the New Israel: our blessed Lord Jesus Christ. As he moved steadfastly to go to Jerusalem to face the enmity and contempt of his foes, he could have said "All these things are against me. All these men of power are against me." He never underestimated the enemy's strength. Even his handful of followers forsook him and fled when the danger deepened. But he knew that he was not alone, that the great God whom he had often brought near to others was on his side, because he was on God's side. He prayed for forgiveness for his enemies and for us all. Then into God's strong and tender hands he committed his Spirit. Ever since Calvary, men and women have known that God suffers with us and for us. God cannot enter more deeply into the tangle and need and despair of our humanity than he has already entered in Jesus Christ. He has known all the mental and physical anguish that we can suffer. This is why not only the apostle Paul, but you and I as well can say with confidence and joy: "If God is for us, who is against us? He who did not spare his own Son but gave him up for us all, will he not also give us all things with him? Who shall separate us from the love of Christ? Shall tribulation, or distress, or persecution, or famine, or nakedness, or peril, or sword? No, in all these things we are more than conquerors through him who loved us" (Romans 8: 31-32, 35, 37).

PRAYER: Thanks be to thee, O God, for thy glorious good news that, when everything seems against us, thou art for us and for our victory over every circumstance and the sins which so easily pull us down. Thanks be to thee, O Lord Jesus Christ, that nothing in life or death need separate us from God's love in thee. Amen.

Break forth new light, O Lord, from out of thy
Holy Word; and when we cannot see the way
before us, let thy Word be a lamp to our feet;
in Jesus Christ. Amen.

ENTER GOD—
WHEN WE NEED TO FEEL GUILTY

SCRIPTURE: "And here is another parable that he told. It was aimed at those who were sure of their own goodness and looked down on everyone else. 'Two men went up to the temple to pray, one a Pharisee and the other a tax-gatherer. The Pharisee stood up and prayed with himself: "I thank thee, O God, that I am not like the rest of men: greedy, dishonest, adulterous; or, for that matter, like this tax-gatherer. I fast twice a week and I set apart one tenth of my whole income." But the tax collector stood in a distant corner scarcely daring to look up at Heaven, and with a gesture of despair, said, "God, have mercy on me, the sinner." It was this man, I tell you, who went home acquitted of his sins, rather than the other. For everyone who sets himself up as a somebody will become a nobody, and the man who makes himself nobody will become somebody'" (Luke 18: 9-14, based upon *The New English Bible,* William Barclay's translation, and Phillips).

The Pharisee in Jesus' story needed to feel guilty. The name "Pharisee" literally means "the separated one." Jewish religious leaders had developed and amplified the Jewish law until it included thousands of petty regulations, covering almost every moment and every situation in life. No ordinary person could engage in everyday work and observe all the regulations. Certain religious leaders called Pharisees, many of them high-principled (although overscrupulous) men, separated themselves from everyday activities so as to be able to observe the many rules. One of the unfortunate results of this separation from the business of the secular world was that they cut themselves off from the rank and file of people. The Pharisees were not villains. They took life with desperate seriousness. They accepted the uncomfortableness of the rigorous life they prescribed for themselves. They were good and they knew it. They were equally sure that everyone else was bad. It is told that a certain Rabbi Simeon had a saying which reduced their attitudes to a parody: "If there are only two righteous men in the world, I and my son are two; if there is only one, I am he."

In Jesus' parable, the Pharisee whom Jesus described stood and prayed in a conspicuous part of the Temple. The standing position was quite all right; this was the normal Jewish posture for prayer. It is as reverent to stand as to kneel, as long as we are consciously in God's presence. But the way in which he stood betrayed his sin of pride and exclusiveness. He wanted to be conspicuous. Worse, when he did pray he prayed *with* himself. Publicly his prayer was one of thanksgiving. Actually, it was a vote of confidence in himself and a motion of self-congratulation. He boasted that he was not a robber, a greedy and unjust man, or an adulterer. He informed God that not only was he morally about as perfect as a man could be, but that he went beyond the call of duty by fasting twice a week. The only obligatory fast for Jews was on the Day of Atonement. As for his support of the Temple he certainly went beyond what was legal and necessary.

In sharp contrast was the other man in this true-to-life story. He was a corrupt tax collector — a grafter and a crook, classed by public opinion together with robbers and murderers. Unlike the respectable Pharisee, he prayed the sinner's prayer, because he knew that he was a sinner and he had honest guilt feelings. "God be merciful to me *the* sinner," he said. The King James Version reads, "*a* sinner" but in the original language it is "*the* sinner." It was as if the tax collector considered himself more of a sinner than anyone else. Today let me make this point: *the tax collector needed to feel guilty, and he did.* He acknowledged his guilt and prayed for mercy. In his crystal-clear humility he was nearer to God than the man who was completely unconscious of any wrongdoing and devoid of any feeling of guilt. He pleaded with God to cleanse him of his stain, and God accepted him. He "went down to his house justified." This does not mean that he went down righteous; rather it means he was accepted — forgiven — by God's grace.

There are times when we need to feel guilty. This view is not shared by some intelligent people. They know from personal experience or from observation of the experience of others that guilt feelings can work havoc in personality. Is there anyone who would not agree that it is a kind of psychological torture to induce feelings of guilt deliberately in a person for trivial failures to measure up to a family code or the negative morality of a harsh religious creed? More than one person has been reduced to a feeling of trembling inferiority by some authority in the family or place of employment who so ruthlessly points out his failings that he says *"I am a complete failure,"* whereas he should say, simply, "I made a mistake and I'm sorry for it."

Therefore, we must say that many guilt feelings are unwarranted, and that to induce in others feelings of guilt for actions which may be only those of immaturity or illness is wrong and less than Christian.

Nevertheless, *there are times when many of us need to feel guilty because we are guilty.* You may think of valid reasons or causes.

(1) *We need to feel guilty when we settle for negative goodness.* This is the kind of goodness exhibited by the Pharisee in Jesus' parable. He congratulated himself on the things he did *not* do. Even his fasting and tithing were negative, in the sense that they represented things which he gave up. One of the chief differences between Jesus' Golden Rule and the similar rule which existed in Judaism and in many other religions consists in its positive quality. The Golden Rule says, essentially, *"Do* unto others as you would have them do unto you" (see Matthew 7:12). The negative idea is found in Judaism and elsewhere, and virtually says "Don't do to others what you do not want them to do to you." The negatively expressed rule is comparatively easy to keep. You simply refrain from doing certain things. At a funeral the clergyman, in paying tribute to a departed friend, said "He was a fine Christian. He didn't smoke, drink, or swear." We assume he didn't steal, lie, or covet his neighbor's wife. These are virtues. But, as one said, they are negative virtues possessed by every fence post. Moses said, "Thou shalt not. . . ." But Jesus added the idea that love is the fulfilling of the law. The positive idea requires us to go "all out" to be kind, helpful, fair, and loving to others as we would have them be to us. Do you think that at the end of life's day in this world God will ask "What did

113

you *not* do"? Isn't it more likely that the Judge and Lover of men will ask, "What *did* you do? What were you able to do to make life easier, kinder, and more worth living for others?"

(2) Another time when we need to feel guilt and to do something about our distressed consciences is *when we commit sins of the spirit.* You have been told more than once that our Lord condemned sins of the spirit, attitudes toward others, more than even the so-called grosser sins of the flesh. He was gentle, patient, understanding, and forgiving towards a prostitute who was dragged into his presence by self-righteous accusers. She was truly penitent, and she was forgiven and reclaimed by the Lord of life into newness of life. He welcomed a penitent thief into Paradise with him. How harsh he was on those whom he called "whited sepulchres" and "the generation of vipers," because they were guilty of greed, injustice, hatred, contempt for the weak and obvious failures. In the story that Jesus told, each of the two men said what he thought about others, his neighbors. The Pharisee despised others. He looked at mankind and thanked God that he was like none of his fellow human beings, whom he pronounced as unworthy and worldly, like this tax collector. The other man stood afar off from other men, such as this uncommonly respectable Pharisee, because he felt unworthy of their friendship.

When you look at this unattractive person in the parable, you can realize the truth in what a Christian realist has written: "All our prejudices of race and class are in the first man, the indifference to widespread wretchedness by which we provoke revolt. Comfortable people do not care how the other half of the world lives, so the neglected turn to bitter cruelty." [1]

Whenever I regard another human being as a thing, and not as a person with rights and needs which God wants me to help him meet; whenever I use a person for my own advantage; whenever I rubber-stamp a person or group as "impossible" or incorrigible, or use a racial name or religious label to downgrade him; whenever I treat a human being as a means to something I may want instead of as an end in himself, I have sinned and need to feel guilty. Then I may turn around — repent — and realize forgiveness.

Is there any worse sin than failure to love with the love that

[1] W. R. Bowie *et. al., Interpreter's Bible,* Vol. 8, p. 309.

knows when to speak and when to be silent, the love thàt is patient, that is not possessive, that is not conceited or rude, that keeps no score of wrongs, that never gloats over the sins of others, that has no limit to its faith, hope, or endurance? (cf. 1 Corinthians 13, as translated in *The New English Bible* and by J. B. Phillips).

(3) Without attempting to list all the failures of which we are often guilty, let me add one more. We who profess and call ourselves Christian are saved to serve. We worship to work. Much church work is Christian work. But much Christian work is not church work. We enter God's house to worship God, the most important activity in which human beings engage. This means the offering of ourselves, our prayers, and our praises, to the great God. His love for us demands such a response. Then we leave God's house more strongly impelled and better equipped to live the life God desires us to live. This may mean thankless involvement in community and world causes. When one of our younger men in the ministry which is devoted to the work of the inner city was asked what the people in a downtown church which held itself aloof from the inner city could do, his answer was direct and clear. "You don't need a specific program or another project. You have a great opportunity to influence the changes needed in the inner city. Why? Because you have in your membership some of the key men and women of the city and county's industrial, business, professional, and educational world." Christians are committed to Christ, and must be involved in the world as Christian business leaders, teachers, factory and store workers, physicians, lawyers, bankers, secretaries, and clerks. If we are not acting as responsible, concerned Christians in our vocations from Monday to Saturday, as concerned, involved Christian citizens every day of the week, we need to feel guilty. God seeks to use our guilt feelings to lead us to repentance, forgiveness, and right-about-face.

In the story, as in life, both the Pharisee and the publican were sinners. Jesus did not approve of the tax collector's way of living; he hated it. Nor did he condemn the Pharisee's charities and integrity. He did condemn the Pharisee's motive and his sins of the spirit. But the tax collector opened his life to God's grace and mercy. Jesus, the supreme authority on such matters, knew that God accepted this humble, honest, guilt-ridden man, who prayed "God, have mercy on me, the sinner." Said Jesus: "It was this man, I tell you, who went home acquitted of his sins, rather than the other." Unacceptable as he was to the smug, satisfied Pharisee, he was accepted by God.

Enter God — when we need to feel guilty. He comes in judgment. He comes in insight into our sins of omission, of spiritual attitude, of separation from our fellow souls, and from our willingness to say "Lord, Lord," and not do what our Lord says.

But *God never enters any life or any community as Judge only.*

> "With mercy and with judgment,
> My web of time He wove,
> And aye the dews of sorrow
> were lustred with his love."

As Jesus Christ was in his earthly life, so God is eternally. Jesus pictured and demonstrated God as always forgiving, and forever hating the sin but loving the sinner. When Simon Peter wallowed and almost sank in waves of guilt feelings as he confronted the Master, he cried, "Depart from me, for I am a sinful man, O Lord!" (Luke 5:8). But Jesus did not let him stay that way. He never does. He said, "Do not be afraid; henceforth you will be catching men" (Luke 5:10). "Follow me," he said to these fishermen. "Follow me and I will *make* you . . . what you have in you to become" (Matthew 4:19; Mark 1:17). We are to accept God's offer, not as encouragement to complacency, but as a release to growth. The tax-gatherer was forgiven, that he might move in the direction of his full potential.

PRAYER: God be merciful to us, sinners. Thou *art* merciful. Thou art steadfast Love, and we know thou canst make us as sure of thy forgiveness as we are of our failures. To someone today who is burdened with anxiety or guilt speak thy liberating Word: "Thou art loved. . . . Thou art accepted. . . .Thy sins are forgiven. Go into peace and freedom and joy." Amen.

O blessed Lord, despite our unworthiness, take
our lips and speak through them, take our
minds and think through them, take our hearts
and set them on fire with thy love; in Christ.
Amen.

ENTER GOD —
WHEN WE ARE AFRAID

SCRIPTURE: "For even when we came into Macedonia, our bodies had no rest but we were afflicted at every turn — fighting without and fear within. But God, who comforts the downcast, comforted us by the coming of Titus, and not only by his coming but also by the comfort with which he was comforted in you, as he told us of your longing, your mourning, your zeal for me, so that I rejoiced still more" (2 Corinthians 7:5-7).

Africans have much wisdom distilled into their sayings. Here is one: "Don't let rats eat your harp strings." Don't let the rats of fear and worry eat your harp strings. Don't let them take away your song.

The apostle Paul had rats eating at his harp strings. In the seventh chapter of his second letter to the Corinthian church he speaks of his distress as a person would confess his deep trouble to an understanding friend. Let me read James Moffatt's translation of Paul's words:

"For I got no relief from the strain of things, even when I reached Macedonia; it was trouble at every turn, wrangling all round me, fears in my own mind. But the God who comforts the dejected comforted me by the arrival of Titus. Yes, and by more than his arrival, by the comfort which you had been to him; for he gave me such a report of how you longed for me, how sorry you were, and how eagerly you took my part, that it added to my delight."

Paul is not indulging in the cheap luxury of self-pity. As a Christian leader and builder of churches he has been having a rough time. In Macedonia where he expected some relief, his body continued to take a beating: "Even when we reached

Macedonia there was still no relief for this poor body of ours" (2 Corinthians 7:5, *New English Bible*). He had no rest. Pain must have been his miserable companion: "We were afflicted at every turn." He speaks of "fighting without," meaning "quarrels all round us." These may well have been attacks from Macedonian foes of the young Christian cause. More serious to him was opposition in one of the important churches which he loved and wanted to strengthen. "Fighting without and fear within," he writes. The fears may have been chiefly related to the situation in the city of Corinth. There can be no doubt that Paul was haunted by anxiety over the situation in that city which occupied a highly strategic position in the Christian movement. Earlier in this same letter the valiant disciple of Christ referred to this anxiety. "When I came to Troas to preach the gospel of Christ, a door was opened for me in the Lord: but my mind could not rest because I did not find my brother Titus there. So I took leave of them and went on to Macedonia" (2 Corinthians 2: 12-13). Paul was deeply concerned about the Corinthians' welfare, and distressed over his estrangement from them. In that section of his letter where he first mentions going to see Titus, we might expect him to tell of the thrilling reunion with his colleague and friend. But his preoccupation with the people in Corinth, whom he loves, diverts him. Instead he spends the next five chapters discussing his ministry as Christ's apostle. The truth seems to be that the man was conscious of his own inadequacy, his aches of memory and gusts of shame.

More men and women, boys and girls than we might suspect have trouble with the rats of anxiety and dread eating away at their harp strings. True, some fears which were recently prevalent have been either dissolved or greatly lessened. Unemployment does remain, and there is such a condition as "Poverty — U.S.A." The Community Chest, the United Fund, the Red Cross, and the County Welfare are still needed, and their services are essential to considerable numbers of human beings in all our cities as well as in many rural districts.

The fears of most of us are in other categories. Always we need to remember that fear is of two kinds, one efficient and beneficial, the other inefficient and destructive. The eighteenth-century British statesman, Edmund Burke, put it this way: "Early and provident fear is the mother of safety." Every time I fly in

118

a plane I am thankful that the pilots have a healthy fear of making an error in takeoff, landing, or in flight. Every time a patient anticipates surgery, he is grateful that the surgeon is afraid of cutting into the wrong places. Who isn't thankful that the pharmacist in the local drug store has a fear of giving the wrong drugs in a prescription? Each of these persons has a healthy fear that makes him efficient. Natural, reasonable, or healthy fears are fears directed to objects which threaten life. Worry is beneficial when it is responsible concern. Every thoughtful citizen, every Christian, must do a certain amount of worrying. Cheap, lazy indifference is perilous.

But the fears which are inefficient are truly destructive of health and usefulness. As Dr. Will C. Menninger of the famous Topeka Clinic has said, "If you get scared, your blood pressure goes up and stays up, without any apparent cause. Anxiety can cause all sorts of more serious physical symptoms without any organic reason for disease." We can think about our problems or we can worry about them. It is said that worry is thinking that has turned toxic.

Paul's fears were not what we would call morbid or unreasonable. He knew also the cure because he knew intimately, through his trusting faith and loving obedience, the one Physician who can heal us when we are afraid. Fear and worry *can* be cured. Robert Louis Stevenson, the nineteenth-century novelist, once suggested that in every human drama there is the stage direction "Enter God." How does God enter when we are anxious and afraid?

First, when we are afraid, God enters to help us face our fears. More than one person has found help by writing down precisely what it is that he has been worrying about. In writing down our fears, or in talking them out with a friend who will listen — a minister, doctor, or other counselor — the fears diminish. Many of them will seem to be baseless. When Chief Justice Oliver Wendell Holmes was in a despondent mood, he found a note on his desk written by his wife: "Dear Oliver: You have lived a long time and have seen many troubles, most of which never happened." Paul knew why he was afraid that something unfavorable might develop in Corinth. Things had gone wrong there. He tried to set them right in a flying visit which only made things worse, and which nearly broke his heart. He then dispatched a trouble shooter — Titus — with a letter which really burned the Corinthians up. Paul was intensely afraid that his severe letter had caused irreparable damage to their relations. They were ready to listen to unfounded charges against him.

Enter God in the next act in the emotional drama that was playing on the stage of Paul's soul. How did God enter into the situation and resolve the fear and dissolve anxiety? Not only by enabling Paul to face all the facts which compounded his fears, but by the coming of a Christian friend. "But God, who comforts the downcast, comforted us by the coming of Titus." With the coming of Titus, Paul's fears were swept away. Titus brought wonderfully good news.

To have a Titus in your life is to be rich indeed. To have someone who knows all about you and who still believes in you, and in your potential, is surely to be among the most fortunate. In the play *Dylan,* based on the life of the poet Dylan Thomas, Sir Alec Guinness marvelously portrays the Welsh genius when he is moving toward his tragic death at the age of thirty-nine. One of the most poignant moments comes when Dylan cries, "God, I am so lonely! I am so lonely!" Present on the stage is his wife, who loves him and whom he loves in a wild kind of way. But, even though he knows of her love and basic loyalty, he needs Another — God. This illustrates the reason why we must surrender all our fears to God, who gives himself to us in Christ and who enters into our innermost situation through the Holy Spirit. This is why we must do more: We must enter into the company of Christ's followers. With all its weaknesses, sins, stuffiness, and tendency to condemn those who fall, the church is still the healing fellowship of the concerned. First, we face our fears. Second, we surrender our fears and anxieties to God. Third, we commit ourselves to Christ, which means that we commit ourselves to the body of Christ, the company of his followers and friends, the living Church. The Church is an imperfect fellowship, an imperfect institution, but it is the one group in which we are more likely to be accepted as we are, in the Spirit of Christ.

Note how the church in Corinth played a major role in banishing Paul's fears and anxieties and, in replacing Titus, driving out discouragement with joy. "But the God who comforts the dejected, comforted me by the arrival of Titus. Yes, and by

120

more than his arrival, by the comfort which you had been to him; for he gave me such a report of how you longed for me, how sorry you were, and how eagerly you took my part, that it added to my delight" (2 Corinthians 7:6-8, Moffatt). God entered through Titus, and through the good news Titus brought to the apprehensive apostle. Titus had evidently been in low spirits when he went on his mission to Corinth. The changed spiritual climate in Corinth gave him a tremendous lift, and Paul shared his joy. Titus knew now that the Corinthians were not "fed up" with Paul; that they were in fact grieving over the wrong they had done the apostle, and were completely committed to defending and satisfying him.

There are those who feel that they can be pro-God and pro-Christ, and yet anti-church. They fail to realize that the great God and gracious Lord to whom they would remain loyal loves the church with all its sins, shortcomings, littlenesses, and stupidities, because the fellowship which is the church is integral to Christian faith and indispensable to spiritual growth.

You and I can decide that we do not intend to live with our fears. You and I can face our fears and anxieties and turn them over to God. You and I can follow our surrender with our commitment to Christ. Such surrender and commitment involve membership in the church. It is within the church that we can find God's agents and instruments.

Confessing our fears, surrendering them to the Christlike God, committing ourselves to Christ, practicing his presence, and becoming involved in his Church provide the surest cure I know for the fears which destroy our peace and could destroy ourselves. Do I hear someone say incredulously, "But surely you can't seriously mean the local church?" I do. "With all its innocuous 'nice' people, with their overemphasis on the trivial and their allergies to the really significant issues of our time?" It is true that many thoughtful persons who are essentially Christian are disenchanted with the local church. But this disillusionment can be a way of deceiving ourselves. One writer says: "Our situation resembles the way in which certain motion pictures are made. Traditionally most films have been made in huge, self-contained Hollywood studios where fake scenery and mocked-up buildings give the appearance of reality. There is a growing tendency, however, to seek for greater realism in films by going

121

on location. This means that the film company leaves the studio in search of real countryside, real towns, real buildings and even real people."[1] Most of us are much more impressed by a film when we recognize that it has been done on location. He continues: "God intends his gospel to be taken on location. And by location [I mean] the local parish. The most real and decisive encounters of the gospel with the world occur in the local church."[2]

Are you afraid for yourself, for one you love, for the future? Are you anxious about your own job? Your own weakness? Are you fearful that your temperament, your personality, will throw you? Do you dread growing old? Are you afraid you will die before you really live? Are you afraid of death? Are you frightened at the thought of losing love? Of having an incurable disease? Of being found out?

"Without were fightings, within were fears" (2 Corinthians 7: 5-6, King James Version). Don't forget that this is followed by the word "nevertheless." "Nevertheless," God who comforts those who are dejected, longs to comfort you by the coming of some Titus, some genuine Christian, and by the support and friendship of a congregation of Christ's church. "Nevertheless God!" Keep on fighting your fears; and the rest will be music and a march to victory.

Recall Jesus' last words from the Cross. He turned to Psalm 31, the so-called going-to-sleep prayer of a child: "Into Thy hand I commit my spirit." This should be not just a final prayer but our daily prayer. It is the prayer for every crisis. "Into thy hand." It is with our hands that we hold things; they signify keeping power. God's hand means his ability to keep us. When we confide ourselves to him, when we commit ourselves, we are kept by him, and have nothing more to fear.

PRAYER: Father, into thy hands we commit ourselves, our dear ones, thy church, our country, and our world. Quietly, confidently, trustfully, we place ourselves into thy hands, through Jesus Christ our Savior. Amen.

---

[1] Lee C. Moorhead, "The Priority of the Local Church" in *The Pulpit* (March, 1964), p. 15. Reprinted by permission.
[2] *Ibid.*

Lead us into deep understanding of thy truth,
O God, that we know the Way, the Truth,
and the Life which are in Christ. Amen.

ENTER GOD —
WHEN WE NEED TO BE CHANGED

SCRIPTURE: "And calling to him a child, he put him in the midst of them, and said, 'Truly, I say to you, unless you turn and become like children, you will never enter the kingdom of heaven'" (Matthew 18:2-3). "Except ye be converted, and become as little children, ye shall not enter into the kingdom of heaven" (Matthew 18:3, King James Version). "Now there was a man of the Pharisees, named Nicodemus, a ruler of the Jews. This man came to Jesus by night and said to him, 'Rabbi, we know that you are a teacher come from God; for no one can do these signs that you do, unless God is with him.' Jesus answered him, 'Truly, truly, I say to you, unless one is born anew, he cannot see the kingdom of God.' Nicodemus said to him, 'How can a man be born when he is old? Can he enter a second time into his mother's womb and be born?' Jesus answered, 'Truly, truly, I say to you, unless one is born of water and the Spirit, he cannot enter the kingdom of God'" (John 3:1-5).

Enter God. This is the stage direction for the great drama of living. *Enter God* when we need to be changed. Enter God — not God "up there" or "out there," but God closer than breathing, as near as our need, the God who came in Jesus Christ and who comes into our lives by the Spirit. Certainly most of us would agree that if we need any radical transformation, a power greater than ourselves must effect it.

But we may not need changing. This may be because we are now moving in the right direction. Goals, motives, resources, all seem to be as good as we could wish. We may not feel any need of change — not because we are in perfect orbit around God, but because we are doing quite well as we are, thank you. Do you recall the sturdy former school teacher, the heroine of the little story of some years ago, "Good Morning, Miss Dove"? She objected to saying the "General Confession" in *The Book of Common Prayer* because of the blunt description in the opening words: "Almighty and most merciful Father; We have erred, and strayed from thy ways like lost sheep." She refused to classify herself as a silly, stupid sheep!

Miss Dove to the contrary notwithstanding, we hesitate to thank God that we are not like other men, in need of drastic change in character, personality, and behavior. Without being split personalities we are sometimes painfully aware of a lower self and a higher self. One part of ourselves may say "Go," and another may be saying "No." A college professor said that he thought there must be two of him, a living soul and a Ph.D.!

There are times when we sense our need for reformation, especially when we are alone, perhaps at night, doing a little honest thinking. Then we may have flashes of insight. If only we could be free from a sense of failure or inadequacy, and from haunting memories! If only we could replace forever that quick temper, that debilitating habit, that low boiling point! Can a drunkard be truly reformed and become sober? Can the egotist become unselfish, can the grouch become genial? Can the individual who is plagued with an unfortunate temperament be helped to integrate his personality and learn the secret of self-mastery? It comes as a rude surprise to realize that what we really need, at least what we are brooding about, is what the Bible calls "salvation." It is from the Greek word *sōtēria*, meaning rescue.

Can human nature be genuinely, radically changed? There are those who answer bluntly, "No." Some believe that any chance of reforming an individual beyond the adolescent period is simply hopeless. By that time our faults of temper and temperament are too deeply embedded in our character to be rooted out and destroyed. Such persons could even quote the Bible in support of their position. Jeremiah, in chapter 13, verse 23, asks: "Can the Ethiopian change his skin or the leopard his spots? Then also you can do good who are accustomed to do evil." This famous verse is not trying to deny freedom of will, or the possibility of repentance. Rather it recognizes the force of custom or habit and early training. The prophet is almost saying that man is born with freedom of choice, but through habit his will may become essentially rigid.

124

Many years ago, the late Dick Sheppard, an Anglican padre much honored and loved, told a story of a man who sat drinking at a bar: "He had been drinking for a long time. . . . As he drank, he wept. He wept because he had wasted his life. He wept because he had failed to do his duty by his family. . . . because he had never appreciated his wife properly. He wept because somehow his good intentions always went wrong. But never mind, he told himself, this time it would be different. He would redeem the past and make up for everything. All, he resolved, would yet be well. He felt uplifted and noble at the very thought. His mind glowed with a genial assurance of virtue. Just then the bartender said, "Time, gentlemen, please.'"[1] It was closing time, and the remorseful man went home and swore at his wife.

Can anything be done for a man like that? His intentions are good; his performances are sad. He wants to be a better man, obviously, but his faults are inveterate. No, say many people who consider themselves realists, and some who are trained in the social sciences. They believe that a philanderer will be a philanderer until the last gun is fired . . . that the drunkard is reformed only in fiction . . . that the grouch becomes sweet-tempered in Pollyanna stories . . . that the miser becomes generous only in dreams of idealists. But we keep on hoping and working for a better world, don't we? Powerful as are the influences of heredity, environment, glands, genes, and the other factors which mold us, we work for a greater measure of justice, dignity, and peace brought about by responsible citizens. Is the world always to be at the mercy of crooks, gangsters, sensualists, exploiters, and bigots? If it is true that human nature will stubbornly resist change for the best, aren't we doomed to disappointment in our hopes for our community, our state, our nation, and our world? Can we avoid our doom? Can man's ethical and spiritual life catch up with his scientific skill? Someone has said that this question is not simply the question of the hour, but the question of the ages.

When we need to be changed, can we be changed? The Christian faith and the experience of innumerable Christians answers in a ringing affirmative. However endemic in humanity evil may

[1] Robert J. McCracken, *Questions People Ask* (New York: Harper & Row, Publishers, 1951), p. 104.

125

be, it is not incurable. There is a remedy. Indeed, there are those who are not within the Christian fellowship and faith who would agree. The basic pattern of human nature can be changed, they say. Such persons differ from Christians chiefly in their view of the way in which the transformation can be effected.

If certain citizens refuse to despair, it is because they place their hopes in *education*. They believe that knowledge can produce a higher race or civilization having the flame of freedom in its soul and the light of knowledge shining in its eyes. If only education can be given a fair chance on a large enough scale, they say, ignorance can be dispelled, prejudice can be overcome, and men and women can be emancipated from much that drags them down. However, educationalists themselves warn us that if education consists wholly of vocational training, or of the development of scientific skills, there will be a tendency to produce young barbarians who have no knowledge of the rich heritage of culture and who are blind outside of their own narrow field of learning. New knowledge can be used to blast rather than to benefit mankind. One eminent educator, Sir Richard Livingstone of Oxford University, has observed that we and our education have been overabsorbed in the matter of life and have not thought of its spirit. He suggests that "we must restore it to a vitamin, deficient both there and in our life — a religion, a philosophy of living, a definite ideal to guide, discipline and dominate the lives of individuals, and through them, national life."

Others feel that when we need to be changed the real force is *legislation*. Let's be fair. In spite of our natural reactions against legalism, we must admit that legislation has a long, impressive list of achievements to its credit. Just because we may take a dim view of the power of legislation in itself to move people into a better society, we would not wish to repeal the Constitution of the United States or make null and void the emancipation of the slaves. And, despite inevitable failures and weaknesses, the United Nations Charter, the rule of law in international relations, is important, if not indispensable, to the settlement of disputes between nations without resorting to violence.

Yet our real need is deeper. It is deeper than education or legislation can reach. We have to use the best system we can devise, but we must get behind the system to the men and women who comprise it. Would you agree with this statement?

"No legal framework, no external organization of society, no school or college curriculum will of itself transform character or guarantee that people who before were competitive and grasping and unprincipled over night become the opposite." [2]

What then is the alchemy by which we can get "golden conduct out of leaden instincts"? Alongside education and legislation we set another force, *regeneration*. This describes the central and tremendous claim of Christianity: that we can be changed genuinely, profoundly, and permanently. As one writer has put it: "If Jesus Christ cannot make character, he can make nothing else." But he can. He has. He does. He has been doing it for over sixty generations.

Hugh Redwood, prominent member of the editorial staff of the London *Daily News*, wrote: "If you should ask me by what authority I talk about the power of Christ to change human nature, I should reply to you simply (and God knows without one word or thought of boasting) because he has changed my nature. I can look anybody in the face today — my friends, my colleagues, and what perhaps, is most difficult of all, the members of my own household and family — and be sure that they know, as I know, that I am really and literally a new creature in Christ Jesus since the day when he came into my life." [3] Another shining example is the author of the hymn "In the Cross of Christ I Glory." Before his conversion to Christ, Sir John Bowring commanded a slave ship. After his transforming experiences he wrote that exultant hymn to the Savior.

This is what Jesus our Lord meant when he said, "Unless one is born anew, he cannot see the kingdom of God." When the cultured and thoughtful Nicodemus asked him how this impossibility could be possible, Jesus explained, "Unless one is born of water and the Spirit, he cannot enter the Kingdom of God." Barclay explains: "The word which the Authorized Version translates *again*, the Greek word *anōthen*, has three different meanings: (i) it can mean *from the beginning, completely, radically*. (ii) It can mean *again*, in the sense of *for the second time*. (iii) It can mean *from above*, and, therefore, *from God*." This phrase

[2] McCracken, *op cit.*, p. 110.
[3] Hugh Redwood, *Residue of Days* (London: Hodder and Stoughton Limited, 1958; and New York: The Macmillan Company, 1959). Reprinted by permission.

in the New Testament carries all three meanings. Barclay further explains: "To be born again is to undergo such a radical change that it is like a new birth; it is to have something happen to the soul which can only be described as being born all over again; and the whole process is not a human achievement, because it comes from the grace and power of God." [4] This idea of rebirth or transformation runs through the New Testament. Sometimes it is spoken of as a death followed by a resurrection, or a re-creation (cf. Romans 6:1-11). Paul speaks of those lately come into the Christian faith as babes in Christ; also, as new creation (cf. 2 Corinthians 5:17; Galatians 6:15). Of course, non-Christian religions also knew this idea. The mystery religions offered the experience of being twice-born. For the Christian this is understood in four closely related ideas: (1) rebirth; (2) the kingdom of God into which a man cannot enter unless he is reborn; (3) the idea of sonship of God through obedience and submission to the Father's will; and (4) eternal life, to possess that kind of life which is the life of God. But being what we are, we are unable to give perfect obedience, to become teachable, open-minded as little children. It is only where the grace of God enters within and changes us that we are able. What do we mean by this phrase? Let Harvard psychologist William James give this now-famous definition of conversion: "The process, gradual or sudden, by which a self hitherto divided, and consciously wrong . . . and unhappy, becomes unified and consciously right . . . and happy, in consequence of its firmer hold upon religious realities." "Born of water and the Spirit," said Jesus. Water is, of course, the symbol of cleansing. Spirit is the symbol of power. God's Spirit enables us to do and be what we cannot be of ourselves. God wipes out the past and gives us victory in the future.

When we feel the need of being changed, what can we do about it? In one sense, nothing: "Nothing in my hand I bring, simply to thy Cross I cling." In another sense we react to God's response to our need. In attempting to explain this question clearly, I feel like the boy whose teacher asked him to write on the subject: "The Funniest Thing I Ever Saw." He wrote, "The funniest thing I ever saw was too funny for words." Right! So

[4] William Barclay, *The Gospel of John*, Vol. 1 in *The Daily Study Bible Series* (Philadelphia: The Westminster Press, 1955), pp. 113-114.

the mind says: The greatest thing I ever saw is too great for words. Transformed personality does not conform to one type, nor is it attained along one road. Some are transformed like the Prodigal Son, in tears and deep repentance. Others come as little children, in naturalness, steady growth, and development. "We have not all sinned alike, but all alike have sinned." Here is a simple way:

(1) *Admit our need to be changed within.*

(2) *Admit our need to have a Power stronger than ourselves to do it.*

(3) *"Enter God" in Jesus Christ through the power of his Spirit,* to help us break radically with our past, our habits, and perhaps with our environment. To repent is not only to change our minds, but to turn around. It means coming up out of the cellar, out of the basement of the house of life, and awakening to a world to which we may have been dead.

Let go of the past and let God now take over. Someone has said it doesn't take time, it takes surrender. A little Chinese girl said to her Christian teacher: "Our gods ask so much. Your God gives so much." He gives himself as gracious, forgiving love.

PRAYER: This is our prayer today, O God of love. Let someone experience now the miracle of thy transforming grace; in Jesus Christ our Savior. Amen.

Open thy Word to our hearts and our hearts to
thy Word, that we may know thee better, and
love thee more. Amen.

ENTER GOD —
WHEN WE OPEN THE DOOR

SCRIPTURE: "Behold, I stand at the door and knock; if any one hears my voice and opens the door, I will come in to him and eat with him, and he with me" (Revelation 3:20).

One of the famous religious paintings of the early twentieth century is "The Light of the World," by William Holman Hunt. He was a founder of what was called the pre-Raphaelite School of artists. Most of us are familiar with the painting through reproductions of the original in colored pictures or stained-glass reproductions. Some of you have seen the original in Keble College, Oxford, England. It shows Christ as a regal figure carrying a lantern and standing before a closed door, knocking. The door is surrounded by weeds and thorns. The door is that of the human soul. Undoubtedly the artist was inspired to create this picture by the words spoken by the exalted Christ in Revelation 3:20: "Behold, I stand at the door and knock: if any one hears my voice and opens the door, I will come in to him and eat with him, and he with me."

As you may know, the artist painted the door with no handle on the outside. The door must be opened from within. The artist is saying to us that the living God in a human personality, Jesus Christ, will not coerce. He will not make himself known until the householder opens the door from the inside. A child to whom a small copy of the painting had been given was fascinated by the symbolism. She brooded about it. She asked her father why the people inside didn't answer the knock and open the door. When no satisfactory answer came from her parent, she offered her own explanation: "I know. They're downstairs in the basement and can't hear him knocking." Sometimes we spend more time in the cellar of life than we should, and we may not hear God knocking at our heart's door. We are immersed with things, and we do not always hear the touch of God upon our lives, our communities, and our church.

But when we open the door and are receptive to what we may call spiritual influences or religious intimations, what then? Is God, who came long ago in Jesus Christ, waiting to enter? And if we invite him, how does he come in? Will God, who came in the historic Jesus of Nazareth, come again in the living Christ? If he is really waiting to enter our lives and beyond all argument and doubt is the most real fact in the universe, the creative Mind and Spirit, personal as well as cosmic, intimate as well as beyond our imagining, will he come in?

The answer to the first question — Is God waiting to enter? — is Yes. This is the answer given by millions, throughout the ages and today. Not all of them claim to be mystical in temperament. Not all of them could claim that they have resolved all doubt. Often they wonder, because they have been exposed to psychology of certain schools, whether this feeling is a kind of wishful thinking on their part, a projection on a cosmic screen.

"Behold, I stand at the door and knock: if any one hears my voice and opens the door, I will come in to him. . . ."

Undoubtedly New Testament scholars and theologians are right in saying that this verse in the book of the prophet John has what they call eschatological meaning. New Testament writers expected the second coming of Christ to take place within their own lifetime. Mark records that Jesus predicted he would not drink again of the fruit of the vine until the day when he would drink it in the kingdom of God (see Mark 14:25). Luke records the warning given to the disciples: "Be like men who are waiting for their master to come home from the marriage feast, so that they may open to him at once when he comes and knocks" (Luke 12:36). This is spiritually true, even if it is not historically true. At moments when we think not, God comes to us. This interpretation is strengthened by Christ, who says that when the door is opened he will come in and eat with the householder. The hope of a banquet with the Messiah was strongly held by devout Jews. In the mind of the writer of this passage, the thought of the second coming of Christ seems to have been dominant.

This does not mean that we may not also interpret this haunting saying in personal, contemporaneous, and mystical ways.

132

Through the power of the Spirit, Jesus Christ is knocking at the door of our hearts. He takes the initiative. As the great French saint Pascal said, "You would not seek him if he had not first sought you." He is the hunger as well as the food. He is not only the answer but the question. He wishes us to welcome him into our personal lives and into our society.

But there is a second question. If we open the door and respond with our love and faith to all that we know of God in Jesus Christ, how will he come?

Certainly he will come in humble, unconventional ways. When he came to Bethlehem he came in strange simplicity. When Christ entered the capital city he certainly came in a way the secular citizen must have thought to be strange for a conqueror. In a modern British passion play a character responds to the first Palm Sunday procession: "A King on a ruddy donkey." When he returned from death he came to those who loved and mourned him in ways that baffled and almost shocked them. Mary supposed him to be a gardener. Thomas was sure that what the other disciples reported from the Upper Room was an illusion and that the one hailed as Risen Lord was an impostor. "Unless I see in his hands the print of the nails, and place my finger in the mark of the nails, and place my hand in his side, I will not believe," said Thomas (John 20:25).

He comes now in strange and surprising ways. A knock on the door of our minds bidding us reach a decision about his claim to be the Savior as well as Teacher and Example, is his way of coming.

Sometimes a call from a fellow human being for help may be Christ himself asking to be welcomed.

When we open the door of our lives, our homes, or our church, he will come in to eat with us. He comes in the sacrament of baptism. He comes in the sacrament of the Lord's Supper. When I was a student I remember that one of the old elders serving communion to us spoke so loudly that we heard him say, "He is as real to me as he was to Peter and John." He comes in our worship as the Real Presence. We go out believing more in him, in ourselves, in the work God has given us to do, and in the future of the world. He comes in Bible study as the Word finds us. He comes in private prayer. Recall the French peasant who prayed silently at the altar of his village church. The *curé,* the pastor, asked him: "What do you say?" "Say?" repeated Pierre, the devout, simple Christian, "I don't say anything. I look at him and he looks at me." "I will sup with him" is the King James translation. To us, supper is not usually the main meal. But the word translated "sup" or "eat" in our English Bibles is the word used for the chief meal of the day. At this meal a man sat and talked for a long time. This is not a mere courtesy call that Christ offers to make. He wants to stay with us. This is precisely what Christ offers to do.

God in Jesus Christ enters when we open the door, and usually he comes to disturb our peace and overturn some things which need to be overturned. His coming may take the form of a jolt to our consciences on some moral question or an ethical issue in our profession or in our political interests. He did that on the Sunday of his last week: "And Jesus entered the temple of God and drove out all who sold and bought in the temple, and he overturned the tables of the money-changers and the seats of those who sold pigeons. He said to them, 'It is written, "My house shall be called a house of prayer"; but you make it a den of robbers'" (Matthew 21:12-13). When we insist on practices which are incompatible with God's kingdom, he upsets our neatly prepared arrangements. The Christ of the Revelation declares "All those whom I love I correct and discipline. Therefore, shake off your complacency and repent" (Revelation 3:19, Phillips). "Behold. . . ."

When we open the door — God enters, in Christ. He comes in ways surprising, humble, and intimate. He comes as a Disturber of conscience. He also comes as Physician, to heal. In Matthew's account of the events of Palm Sunday and Jesus' last week, immediately after telling of Jesus' visit to the Temple he adds: "And the blind and the lame came to him in the temple, and he healed them" (Matthew 21:14).

When we open the doors of our temples, both of the inner sanctuaries of our lives and the sanctuary of our church, *he comes to heal.* How often we need the eyes of our minds and souls opened to the meaning of life, the reality of God, the mighty acts of God in our "creation, preservation, and all the blessings of this life," and above all, to our redemption through the death and victory of our Lord Jesus Christ! How often our spirits are lamed, hurt, and crippled by our own follies and failures! Moreover, spiritual sickness is often a contributing factor to physical illness. Conversely, as our spirits are healed of doubt, resentment, guilt, and despair, our bodily health improves. But even if we must live with some disability, Christ imparts his own strength. We realize what the New Testament means when it speaks of being "strengthened with might through his Spirit in the inner man" (Ephesians 3:16), because Christ dwells in our hearts through faith.

"Behold, I stand at the door and knock: if any one hears my voice and opens the door, I will come in to him and eat with him, and he with me."

PRAYER:
O Lord, with shame and sorrow
  We open now the door;
Dear Savior, enter, enter,
  And leave us nevermore. Amen.

*Let our hearts burn with love within us as thou
dost open to us the Scriptures and give to us
thyself: in Christ our Lord. Amen.*

ENTER GOD — IN THE SHADOWS

SCRIPTURE: "May he strengthen you, in his glorious might, with ample power to meet whatever comes with fortitude, patience, and joy; and to give thanks to the Father who has made you fit to share the heritage of God's people in the realm of light.

"He rescued us from the domain of darkness and brought us away into the kingdom of his dear Son, in whom our release is secured and our sins forgiven. He is the image of the invisible God. . . . He is . . . the first to return from the dead, to be in all things alone supreme" (Colossians 1:11-15, 18, *The New English Bible*).

The women were there watching. They were weeping. They were waiting. And it was a good thing, too. Without that watching, weeping, and waiting in the shadows they might never have been transferred ("translated" is the old word) into the marvelous light of Christ's resurrection.

Enter God. Into the shadows of death, of his cause, and of hope. "Mary stood at the tomb outside, weeping. . . . 'Why are you weeping?' . . . 'If it is you, sir, who removed him, tell me where you have laid him, and I will take him away.' Jesus said 'Mary!' She turned to him and said, 'Rabboni!' (which is Hebrew for 'My Master')" (John 20:11, 13, 15-16, *The New English Bible*).

If you had been faking the story of Jesus' resurrection, you wouldn't have written about it as the Gospel writers did. If you had been inventing a story like that, you'd have done it more dramatically; you would have made it more startling. You wouldn't have it happen quietly in the early morning before anybody was up and around, so that only a few concerned people heard about it in hushed whispers. Wouldn't it really have been more effective to take a leaf from the notebooks of the big producers in Broadway, Hollywood, and Europe and make this tremendous event happen in broad daylight, in full view of crowds of people, and certainly so that the Roman Governor Pilate, and the ecclesiastical top brass such as Caiphas could be overwhelmed by it? Thunder, lightning, and perhaps even an earthquake would liven up the script. But this quiet garden, with frightened, sobbing women finding the stone door rolled away from the tomb; Peter and John, not a host of people, finding grave-clothes lying on the ledge; Jesus walking toward one of the Marys, seeming to her for all the world like a gardener; and the risen Lord coming to the disciples in that secret upper room where they huddled behind bolted doors! "Enter God." The shadows of doubt, despair, bereavement, death, and fear are dissolved as in a burst of burning sunlight. Those first followers of Christ were changed dynamically and in depth, every single one of them. Instead of sneaking off to escape their enemies, they went around in broad daylight saying openly that Jesus Christ was alive again and, of all things, saying it to people who had watched him die and seen him buried. They knew well the risks of talking like that. The very men who "ran scared" on Good Friday were pestered, persecuted, and hounded to death because they persisted in telling the world that Jesus Christ, who had suffered crucifixion under Pontius Pilate, had risen again.

Yes, said Paul, who had experienced the risen Lord long after the first Easter; yes, God "rescued us from the domain of darkness and brought us away into the kingdom of his dear Son, in whom our release is secured and our sins forgiven." You Colossians, he wrote, ought to "give thanks to the Father who has made you fit to share the heritage of God's people in the realm of light."

But it's two thousand years later, now. Two thousand years of history lie between us and the resurrection. The powers of darkness seem to be having a field day, even in our own favored nation in what a recent writer called the second decade of our greatest affluence. To a majority of our contemporaries, Easter is a kind of lyrical interlude; but it's all a bit of the stuff of which dreams are made: a lovely legend, a myth in the everyday meaning of myth. They would make their own the confession of a nineteenth-century poet, Arthur H. Clough, written in Naples, Italy, one Easter Day: "This is the one sad Gospel that is true, Christ is not risen."

138

But God comes, as God came decisively in the resurrection. We can't tidy up all the details of the New Testament accounts of it. We cannot present evidence which will prove it scientifically. If you are determined to disbelieve it, you will be unmoved by the testimonies of eyewitnesses.

"Enter God" in the shadows of doubt and unbelief. Here certainly in the resurrection of Christ, is mystery, not only a problem. Here is the tremendous claim that life came from death, that life came through death. We just cannot remain neutral about it. Bluntly, and harshly, Paul told the Corinthians: "If Christ was not raised, your faith has nothing in it" (1 Corinthians 15:17, *New English Bible*). Perhaps this seems to be laying it on a little too thickly. Some fine-living people could say that they believe in God and put their trust in God through the Jesus who came at Christmas and who died a sacrificial death on Good Friday. They cannot accept full Christianity, but they are certainly the equivalent of committed Christians. They hope that the resurrection faith can be proved true. Do they know that there would be no Christian faith without faith in the resurrection? There would be no living church without conviction in the risen and living Lord whose spiritual body is now the church. If we detach Christ's V-Day from his D-Day; that is, settle for his life, teachings, and death apart from his victory over evil and death in the resurrection, Christ becomes chiefly a past influence, an example, with decreasing influence upon our complex modern world. Most men don't live by faith, but by reason. Some say that Christ is dead. They say that the Syrian stars look down on his grave. No! says the convinced and not always unintelligent or wishful Christian: "Now is Christ risen. The Lord is risen indeed."

How does God enter the shadows of doubt and disbelief? He enters as the Holy Spirit always does, as Guide, Truth, Power, and with the gift of faith. To journey out of darkness into the light of assurance is a journey of faith in its deepest meaning. How can we receive such a faith? One step obviously is to believe in the God of holy, righteous love, who acts in history and in this life, and who steps into human life most clearly in Jesus Christ. Another step is surely to be persuaded that Christians are generally reliable. Has this conviction that Christ defeated death made Christians better? What is the quality of Christian life? Can Christians march on, never doubting that right will triumph? What do you make of the church, its life, witness, worship, and service? With all its sins — with all *our* sins, ineptitudes, littleness, and moral cowardice — it *is* the body of Christ. Today Jesus points to his body the church — Orthodox, Roman Catholic, Protestant — and says, as he did to skeptical Thomas: "Reach your hand here and put it into my side." In other words, test the reality of this body, this fellowship of mine: be unbelieving no longer, but believe (see John 20:27, *The New English Bible*).

"Enter God" — *into the shadows and darkness made by our moral failures; into what the Bible calls sin.* Says Paul to the Colossian church as he combats their heresy that Christ is at best only partially able to provide complete deliverance from the powers of darkness: "He has delivered us from the dominion of darkness and transferred us to the kingdom of his beloved Son, in whom we have redemption, the forgiveness of sins." By his entering in, God "has qualified us to share in the inheritance of the saints in light." The very word translated "qualify" means "to make worthy." God not only gives us the honor, but he also makes us worthy to receive it. A new relationship exists between God and man. When any one puts his trust in Christ, he is delivered from the darkness of guilt, a sense of failure, and from despair. Reinhold Niebuhr, American theologian, once said that forgiveness is the final form of love. God's forgiveness and acceptance of us when we are truly sorry for what we have done and for what we have been and are now, are made real and effectual for us and in us by the living Lord, whom death could not hold. A young pastor was asked one night by a poorly dressed girl if he was a minister. "Yes," he answered. "Would you come then and get my mother in?" she asked. Thinking it was a case of a drunken parent he suggested that it might be better to call a policeman. "Oh, no," said the girl, "my mother's dying, and I want you to get her in . . . into salvation, or whatever it is." The minister went with her into the slum tenement where her mother lay dying. He sat down and talked about the beautiful example of Jesus, of his teaching, and of his spirit. "That's no good, Mister, no good for the likes of me. I'm a poor sinner, and I'm dying." The pastor realized that he had no Good News. Then he thought of the simple truths his own mother had taught

140

him, and he told the old ever-new story of God's love in Jesus Christ. He told the woman that God was in Christ, loving her and everyone so much that he died a hard death and came alive after death to do something that no one else could do. The woman's eyes brightened: "Yes, now you're getting at it. That's for me." The pastor loved to add when he told about it: "I got her in, and I got myself in too." You are no longer at the mercy of the powers of darkness in your life. Your sins have been forgiven. You are free. It wasn't cheaply won for you. It is the most costly gift anyone, including God, can give. The price was the life of God's well-beloved Son.

Enter God — *into the shadows of death, to lead us through the darkest valley of all into his marvelous light of life eternal.* In this first chapter of the Colossian letter the apostle gives us his interpretation of Christ and his place and work in the total scheme of things. Christ is God manifest, the *eikōn,* the image, the picture, of the invisible God. He is in time and dignity prior to all creation. Somehow he holds all things together. Christ is the head of the church, his body. Then Paul declares that he is death's first conqueror, the sovereign Lord of a great risen host. "He is the beginning, the firstborn from the dead" (Colossians 1:18). He is "the first to return from the dead, to be in all things alone supreme. For in him the complete being of God, by God's own choice, came to dwell" (Colossians 1:18-19, *New English Bible).* When a young person dies, or a useful person of any age, what do we say? We complain that it isn't fair; it isn't right. This is the Christian conviction about death. Death isn't fair; death isn't right. Paul said death is the last enemy. Isn't it still the enemy? Death floors us. If we believe that death is the end, we live in a Good Friday world. The Christian religion did not cross centuries and frontiers because it preached death or a dead Christ. It preached resurrection, a shout of triumph. Death is an enemy, but it will be destroyed. That is why Easter is a full pipe organ, trumpets, alleluias, hosannas, cheers, and hurrahs! God has banished the shadows of death's power. Alleluia!

PRAYER: Thanks be to thee, Eternal God, that out of earth's darkest hour thou didst bring the dawn; that infinitely stronger than the darkness of evil and death is *thy* power and love. De-

141

liver every soul now living in the gloom of fears or doubt, of loneliness or sorrow, into the marvelous light of thy presence and victory; through Jesus Christ thy Son our Savior and Lord. Amen.

Dear God, help me to speak as I ought to speak, and help those who listen to hear as they ought to hear, that we both, speaker and listener, may receive the truth and obey it, in Christ our Lord. Amen.

WHO WANTS TO LIVE FOREVER?

SCRIPTURE: "Praise be to the God and Father of our Lord Jesus Christ, who in his mercy gave us new birth into a living hope by the resurrection of Jesus Christ from the dead! The inheritance to which we are born is one that nothing can destroy or spoil or wither. It is kept [reserved] for you in heaven, and you, because you put your faith in God, are under the protection of his power until salvation comes — the salvation which is even now in readiness and will be revealed at the end of time" (1 Peter 1:3-5, *The New English Bible*).

Not too long ago I went to a funeral home to make arrangements for the funeral service of a good woman. Her husband of many years was present in the funeral home. He and his wife lived outside our community. Although his wife had been ill for a long time, her death left him truly bereaved. Courteously, he drew me aside from other persons present to ask me this question: "Do you believe that there is anything more after death? Is there a heaven for good people?" He explained why he asked me the question privately. "I have heard," he said, with unexpected gentleness, "that many of you clergy do not believe what you are expected to believe. I will respect your answer. But do you believe there is anything after death?" I answered him truthfully. "Yes," I said, "I do believe that there is a life beyond this life. I do not have any more inside information about it than any other human being. But I believe there is for the Christian, and perhaps for many others who do not come to God in the Christian way, something we call 'heaven.' When my own doubts assert themselves and I am tempted to think that biological death has the last word, I put my confidence in Christ. He is at least the supreme authority on life and death."

143

Today I make no apology for speaking on this theme. True, it is often supposed that modern ministers of religion avoid sermons on death and the Christian belief in eternal life. We are reported to avoid these themes because we do not wish to be considered otherworldly. After all, the church must "get with it," get with the secular city, and extend the church's witness and ministry deep into this real world of here and now. A threadbare sneer at Christians is the old cliché: "Religion preaches pie in the sky bye-and-bye." Certainly the living church must concern itself with the evils and possibilities of life as it is lived now. Interestingly it has been written: ". . . The Christians who did most for the present world were just those who thought most of the next. The Apostles themselves, who set on foot the conversion of the Roman Empire, the great men who built up the Middle Ages, the English Evangelicals who abolished the Slave Trade all left their mark on Earth because their minds were occupied with Heaven." [1] Moreover, we live in a death-denying culture. We push death out of sight as long as we can. In any case, death also is a fact. It is inescapable and unavoidable, and we must come to terms with it.

A central conviction of the Christian church, basic to the teaching of the New Testament, is that for *the one who puts his trust in the God disclosed in Jesus Christ, there is life unbroken by the experience of biological or bodily death.*

The early Christians faced persecution and other pressures. When you pick up the little first letter of Peter, you realize that already the storm clouds are gathering. Nero is on the imperial throne. Christians will be among his victims. There must have been a burdensome sense of insecurity. So Peter (or one who proudly borrows the great apostle's name), writes this letter to steady the shaking knees. Does he begin by offering sympathy? Does he begin by saying, "My heart goes out to you under your great trials, but don't worry, it may never happen?" No; he begins with a resounding ascription of praise and thanks to God: "Blessed be the God and Father of our Lord Jesus Christ!" The "Blessed be" followed by the name of God was a characteristic of Jewish prayer. Peter does not want anyone to misunderstand him. It is the God who has made himself known in Jesus Christ.

[1] C. S. Lewis, *Christian Behaviour* (New York: The Macmillan Company, 1944), p. 55.

The Big Fisherman will have nothing to do with misty religion-in-general. In the first three verses the name of Jesus Christ occurs three times.

God should be thanked for many things, but Peter goes directly to the chief blessing. He thanks God for what he has done for us in Jesus Christ.

What has God done, that we should praise him? What God has done for us in Christ is beyond anyone's power to put into words. Even though what's best worth saying cannot be said verbally, he must try to do it.

"Praise be to the God and Father of our Lord Jesus Christ, who in his mercy gave us new birth." We have undergone a radical transformation — something decisive. We have been born again into a living hope. His words are "new birth into a living hope." And the cause of it, the decisive turning point, was Christ's resurrection.

When God raised Jesus Christ from the dead on the first Easter, God transformed, radically changed, the whole situation for mankind. This tremendous, mysterious fact was the center and secret of the apostle's preaching, the vitality, the triumph, and the certainty of the early church. True, we may distinguish two "moments" in God's action in our spiritual rebirth: that of Christ's resurrection and also the moment when a particular person is made a member of Christ's body, when one spiritually shares in Christ's death, burial, and resurrection. It would seem as if Peter is thinking of baptism, in which the two moments are sacramentally and symbolically one. This action of God opened up a new world of unexpected splendor and enduring beauty. Why enduring? Because those early Christians were like mountain climbers who made their way through heavy mists and fogs until suddenly they were on the summit, with clouds dispersed and glorious sunlight irradiating a wide expanse of wonderful country they had never seen before. They were begotten, born anew, into a living hope that life with Christ would be life forever. Their most distinguishing characteristic in marked contrast to their pagan neighbors was hope.

"Praise be to the God and Father of our Lord Jesus Christ, who in his mercy gave us new birth into a living hope by the resurrection of Jesus Christ from the dead! The inheritance to which we are born is one that nothing can destroy or spoil or wither. It is kept [reserved] for you in heaven, and you, because you put your faith in God, are under the protection of his power."

This inheritance is in heaven. It is eternal. It is not a part of this world which changes, decays, and vanishes. It awaits you, and you will be guarded by God's power until you enjoy the whole sum of what God has in store for you. The future brings joy now. For you may live forever.

But who wants to live forever? Many could say, "Not I!" For some, this life is enough. Sometimes they feel like this because all they know of living has been unsatisfactory, even tragic, a dead end, a burden. Others feel that to go on living even under better conditions is unnecessary. This has been a good life; they have pitched it high. When death comes, it will be because death comes to all living things. A Roman Catholic priest whose parish is in a slum of Liverpool, England, spent three days in a beautiful home with delightful grounds in California. As he said goodbye to his host, he said, "It's perfectly wonderful here. I don't know how you are going to appreciate heaven."

". . . life in our affluent society, with its labor-saving devices and its gadgets to amuse us, no longer seems a 'desert drear'. It is no 'vale of toil and tears' through which we make our weary pilgrimage, moaning, 'O land of rest, for thee I sigh.' It is so filled with interest and excitement we have little time in our busy schedules to focus attention on the life to come." [2]

Who wants to live forever? This question could be asked by those who strongly doubt that any life beyond this life exists or is possible. True, some of these honest skeptics keenly regret that there is not more life available for those who die in infancy, childhood, the morning years of youth, and young adulthood. It seems so unjust that congenital weakness, a disease germ, a bullet, a bomb fragment, or a skidding tire should have the last word, and the last word should be *Finis — The End.*

Many persons feel that to want to go on living forever is a kind of disguised egotism. In any case, a large percentage of persons disbelieve in immortality. Many of them, like the Sadducees in ancient Israel, believe in God, but not in any future life.

However, there are others who wish they could believe in what

[2] William B. Ward, *After Death, What?* (Richmond: The John Knox Press, 1965), p. 73.

the Christian church calls eternal life, provided the next dimension of existence is at least as exhilarating as the best of life has been for them thus far. They would like to live forever if they could be assured of opportunities to grow in knowledge, usefulness, adventures of service, and love. Sir Wilfred Grenfell of Labrador wrote from his bleak mission hospital: "I am very much in love with life. I want all I can get of it. I want more of it after the incident called death, if there is any to be had." This may be our verdict, too. For any person who accepts Christ's interpretation of life, it is easy to fall very much in love with life. We want all we can get of it. We want more of it after the incident called death.

This is not necessarily egotistical or selfish. It may also include the longing that someone with whom we have been very much in love will not be forever ended when his or her body is dissolved. As John Baillie once said, it is hardly likely that when death comes to someone we love very much we can bring ourselves to say as we look at the silent form from which the personality has gone, "For all I know *or* care, this is the end of you my dear!"[3] As Dr. Robert James McCracken once expressed it, "It is when love takes full possession of our hearts that the desire for immortality is strongest. Love cannot brook final separation or endure the thought of extinction." So the Christian reformer and writer Charles Kingsley felt. After his death and not long before his wife's own death, she had inscribed on his tombstone the Latin words which say, "We have loved. We love. We shall love."

Does someone protest: "But honestly now, can you really want to live beyond physical death in the kind of heaven pictured in the Bible? Do you really wish to spend eternity in a white robe, wearing a crown, strumming a harp, and singing hymns interminably, even if the streets are made of gold and the heavenly city's gates are made of pearl?" My answer is, "No; I do not believe in that kind of heaven either." But how wrong, even silly, it is to treat literally the glorious imagery of the Bible! Such images and pictures are Eastern writers' efforts to express the inexpressible. "White robes are symbols of stainless purity, crowns of moral victory, harps of abounding happiness,

[3] John Baillie, *And the Life Everlasting* (New York: Charles Scribner's Sons, 1933), p. 63.

gold of timelessness of heaven — gold does not rust — and of the preciousness of it." [4] Don't we all want stainless integrity, moral victory, abounding joy, and enduring love forever?

Consider then what the Christian hope includes. It is not just never-ending existence, devoid of challenge, achievement, and adventure. Eternal life through Christ cannot be infinite boredom and monotony. It will be a life that has not only continuity but quality. It will not be more of the same; it will be better. Christians should never think of immortality (eternal life is the better phrase) in terms of duration only. What Christians mean by eternal life is life without limitations, no longer subject to conditions of time. What the old English version of our Lord's words about "many mansions" means is "infinite realms where there are new truths to find, new beauties to enjoy, new personalities to know." Do you remember the words of J. M. Barrie in *Peter Pan?* "To die will be an awfully big adventure." Harvard psychologist and professor William James once said that he felt a practical need for immortality. He was asked why, and answered, "Because I am getting fit to live." Even if you live to be one hundred and retain full possession of all your faculties, it will not be long enough for complete fulfillment. Each one has an unfinished symphony to complete. The hope which Christ's resurrection creates in us is that in the life to come all that inhibits our growth here, cripples our personalities, and frustrates our best purposes will be done away. We shall find ourselves in a better environment. As Paul wrote, "I am sure that he who began a good work in you will bring it to completion at the day of Jesus Christ" (Philippians 1:6).

What will it be like? No one this side of death knows, but there are clues in the Bible. *There will be rest,* not rest from labor but rest in labor. "I will give you rest," Christ promised (Matthew 11:28). "There remains a sabbath rest for the people of God" (Hebrews 4:9).

There will be work to do. "These are they who have come out of the great tribulation. . . . Therefore are they before the throne of God, and serve him day and night within his temple . . ." (Revelation 7:14, 15). The word translated "serve" may also be translated "worship," the work of the people.

[4] Robert J. McCracken, "Easter! But Who Wants to Live Forever?" *The Presbyterian Outlook,* Vol. 140, No. 14, p. 5.

Christ will be there. "I will come again and will take you to myself, that where I am you may be also" (John 14:3).

There will be joy, deep and unquenchable. "What no eye has seen, nor ear heard, nor the heart of man conceived, what God has prepared for those who love him" (1 Corinthians 2:9).

There will be enriching fellowship. We had better get ready for complete integration! "After this I looked and saw a vast throng, which no one could count, from every nation, of all tribes, peoples, and languages, standing in front of the throne and before the Lamb" (Revelation 7:9, *The New English Bible*).

There will be reunion with those whom we loved and lost in the midst of the years. Said Jesus, "There are many dwelling-places in my Father's house; if it were not so I should have told you" (John 14:2, *New English Bible*). Our Father's home means that all the family will be there, certainly all who early or late put their trust and love in God and their fellowmen. Going there will not be entering a foreign land when day is done. It will be *going home.*

There will be peace. It will be indestructible, the peace after pain, the peace following struggle, God's peace. "He will wipe away every tear from their eyes, and death shall be no more, neither shall there be mourning nor crying nor pain any more" (Revelation 21:4).

How can we know whether this is wishful thinking? Fact or fantasy? We cannot know with absolute finality. But one thing is sure, no fact discovered by modern scientists makes the biblical teaching on eternal life impossible or improbable.

On what do we base our faith? Chiefly on two of the most significant truths we know.

First, we base our faith on the idea that Professor Ian Ramsay of Oriel College, Oxford, England, calls *"cosmic self-disclosures."* *These are God's self-revelation of his character and purpose.* I believe in the resurrection of the body — the renewal of the personality in a spiritual body — and the life everlasting because of all that we know of God.

> "To one fixed trust my spirit clings;
> I know that God is good!" [5]

Said Nobel prizewinning physicist Dr. Arthur H. Compton, some-

[5] From John Greenleaf Whittier, "The Eternal Goodness."

time of California Institute of Technology: "As long as there is in heaven a God of Love, there must be for God's children everlasting life. This is not the cold logic of science but the warm faith of a father who has seen his child on the brink of death." [6]

The other foundation of faith in life eternal is *what we know of Jesus Christ.* Because he conquered death, we know that what he taught and implied concerning life is true. It is this tremendous fact and faith that enabled a twentieth-century saint to write to a friend:

"My dear Findlay and wife: To my surprise I have just been told that my days and hours are numbered. It may be that, before this reaches you, I shall have gone to the Palace. Don't trouble to write. *We shall meet in the morning.* With much love, Yours affectionately, F. B. Meyer"

PRAYER: O God, we most heartily thank thee that when our Lord Jesus Christ had conquered death he opened the kingdom of heaven to all believers. Amen.

[6] Arthur H. Compton, "A Scientist on Immortality," in *The Golden Book of Immortality,* Thomas Curtis Clark and Hazel Davis Clark, eds. (New York: Association Press, 1954), pp. 54-55.

Stab our minds and spirits broad awake, O
Holy Spirit, that we may receive and obey thy
word for us today; in Christ. Amen.

GOING TO CHURCH!
YOU CAN'T BE SERIOUS!

SCRIPTURE: "And he came to Nazareth, where he had been brought up; and he went to the synagogue, as his custom was, on the sabbath day" (Luke 4:16). "So he came to Nazareth, where he had been brought up, and went to synagogue on the Sabbath day as he regularly did" (Luke 4:16, *The New English Bible*).

The conversation could have taken place in a dormitory at any university, college, or school. My friend the Reverend Melvin E. Wheatley of the Westwood Community Methodist Church in Los Angeles, in his sermon of September 18, 1966, says it occurred at one of the fine California colleges. It was reported by the chaplain. A troubled freshman came to him for counseling. On her first Sunday at school that fall she had risen bright and early and had begun to dress. Her roommate was an upper-class member. When the roommate realized that the girl was dressing to go out, she sleepily inquired where she was going. Innocently enough the freshman replied, "I'm going to church." The shocked roommate sat bolt upright in bed. With complete sincerity and total disdain she exclaimed: "Going to church! You can't be serious!"

The college chaplain quickly explained that the roommate's exclamation was not a question; it was an accusation. She was trying to get through to the freshman that a considerable number of college students considered that going to church, any church, was not just the mark of a kind of naive idiot but practically the act of a traitor. She was implying that an enlightened and sophisticated member of the educated younger set in the 1960's considered attendance at church service to be a form of immature dependence; that churchgoing and participation in worship might actually do harm. It supports an outworn superstition.

It puts you in the same category as stuffy, reactionary supporters of the status quo. It identifies you with the kind of pharisaical types who refuse to rebel against what ought to be abolished in our culture if we are to "get with it" in the age of the Pill, space exploration, situation ethics, and protest. Going to church! You can't be serious!

We may get exercised about so-called revolting youth. One of them ticked us off properly when John Lennon of "Beatle" fame observed that the Beatles were more popular in today's world than Jesus. A teen-ager, one of thousands who wrote to newspapers defending John Lennon and his fellow Beatles said that the only ones that he or she had met that were upset by John Lennon's remark were adults. The teen-ager felt like asking all of these people, "If you're so concerned about everyone's religion why aren't you in church every Sunday?" Such an honest question deserves a straight answer.[1]

In spite of the fact that in many communities it is not the "in" thing to go regularly to the public worship of God in church, there are considerable numbers of responsible, fairly normal persons who take the church seriously and who go to church with a high degree of faithfulness. True, the so-called "noise of solemn assemblies" strikes many as being fatuous and irrelevant to the crucial issues of today. True also, there is much faithlessness among us who are members of the visible church. True, there are many abuses of the ethic and total gospel of Christ on the part of clergy and laity. We who are within the church, giving our lives to it, are more aware of our corporate weaknesses, futilities, and sins than even the severest critic on the outside. But there are those who are utterly serious, and they include young people and men and women concerned about better government, more wholesome communities, social justice, more adequate education for all children, replacement of slums by decent housing, and replacing war with peace and justice. Perhaps some of those who are serious about the church and who are serious about participation in the worship of God as often as they possibly can are the new rebels! The conformists may be those who go along with the crowd which couldn't care less

[1] A fair analysis of "The Revolting Students" will be found in Robert McAfee Brown's article of that title in *Presbyterian Life*, November 15, 1966.

about what they sneeringly call conventional, or middle-class church characters.

If you are serious about the church and your participation in its worship, you are in excellent company. The Founder of Christianity supported *regularly* the church of his people and of his time. Was it because he was blind to its weaknesses, its limitations, and the insincerities and downright sins of some of its prominent members and leaders? Indeed he was not! Who was it who lacerated prominent persons with abrasive language — "offspring of vipers," "whited sepulchres," "hypocrites" — but our Lord Jesus Christ? But says Luke in his Gospel: "He went to the synagogue, as his custom was, on the sabbath day." As Luke's Greek is translated in *The New English Bible:* "So he came to Nazareth, where he had been brought up, and went to synagogue on the Sabbath day as he regularly did." Many things in the Temple and the synagogue (as we would say, in church) must have irritated him. Many things must have made him disagree. Some things made him furious. The worship of the synagogue, like the worship of the church today, was far from perfect. Yet Jesus never failed to join himself to God's worshiping people on God's day. Moreover, just as we have laymen in some churches who read one of the Scripture lessons in the service, he, too, participated. But there was this difference: his message rocked his hearers.

Going to church, and taking it seriously means that we know that the worship of God is the priority of the Christian life. Unfortunately some of our sincere and conscientious advocates of having the church extend its ministry into the world, which always has been an imperative, sometimes give the impression that you can separate witness from worship. The more radical among them feel they must be committed to a nonreligious, noninstitutional kind of religion, a so-called "secular" gospel. Assuredly the twentieth-century church invites and deserves criticism. Too often the Word of the Lord is muted by success-conscious officials and organization-minded ecclesiastics. All too often the blind are leading the blind, and perplexed pastors are *following* parishioners. But history shows one heartening fact: Never does the church sink so low and become so ineffectual that it is without what the Scriptures call "a saving remnant." The body of Christ, however weak or maimed, is never a dead body. Look at the

153

Roman Catholic Church. It fashioned feudalism, but it did not die with the passing of feudalism. Look, too, at the Eastern Orthodox Church, which appears to be healthier now under the Communist regime than it has been for ages; it was once tied in with the Czarist state. Down through the centuries revival, sometimes in the form of a group breaking off from the formalism of an established church, has given a new thrust to Christ's ministry and moved creatively into the world. As Daniel Jenkins, no tame apologist for the church, has said, *"The strange thing about the Church is not that it grows old, but that it seems to have discovered the secret of being born again."* [2]

To maintain the idea that worship is all that matters is heretical. To say that our witness in the world is all that matters is heretical. Worship and witness, or service in the world, are inseparable. The church is the body of Christ and it renews its life at the Source of life, God. Listen to this description of what goes on here and in churches of every order and name throughout the earth:

"In the hour of worship the drama of salvation is reenacted, the Event of God-in-Christ is focused on the screen of contemporary life, the holy God confronts man in his sin, and, baring a Father's heart, bids him come home. Christ himself comes to worshiping man in the Word through the human activities of preaching and teaching and in the earthly materials of the sacraments. Some worshipers are indifferent. Others are moved to accept Christ as Lord and Savior. Those who acknowledge their need and accept God's redemptive act respond with confession, hymns of praise, and the giving of themselves to Christ. They go out to sin again and know it. But they also go out to witness — one to face a beguiling temptation with new insight; another to stand alone in some significant controversy because his conscience is captive to the Word; and still another to cope heroically with the newfound knowledge of a killing disease. The 'new community' is at work in the world. Those who worship, witness." [3]

So we go to church and are serious about it (not always solemn) because Jesus found it necessary and desirable; because

[2] Daniel T. Jenkins, *The Strangeness of the Church* (Garden City, N.Y.: Doubleday & Company, Inc. 1955), p. 14.
[3] Fisher, *op. cit.*, p. 105.

the church is not just another human society. It is God's idea and work. The church is the people of the new covenant and as such is no accidental element in the Christian faith. The church is a basic part of the divine purpose, willed by God. It was brought to do God's work in the world. Human beings will worship something or someone: corporation, political leader, machines, money, power, science, or status. This is our human nature. Until man worships the true God, he will engage in all sorts of monkey business, skullduggery and downright demonic acts. Moreover, until he finds himself and learns who he is, he is lost.

This is why we say, *Going to church? Yes. And we are serious about it.* We cannot but be serious, because in worship of God, and in witness to Christ's way, truth, and life where we live, love, work, play, and vote, *we lead an examined life.* The naturalist John Burroughs said that he went to church to find himself. It is so easy to get lost in the world. Isn't it easy? You say it depends on what you mean by the word "lost." Today, unlike the hell-fire-and-damnation yesterdays, a person is punished not because he is lost. He is punished by being lost. A thoughtful man, a Christian who takes church seriously, made a helpful description of what it means today to be lost. "In our time — an individual may be said to be lost if (1) he does not know *who* he is — he lacks a sense of identification; (2) he does not know *where* he is — he lacks a sense of *orientation;* (3) he does not know *where* he wants to be — he lacks a sense of *motivation;* or (4) knowing who he is, where he is and where he would like to be — he yet does not have the vaguest notion of how to get there — he has no sense of *direction.*" [4]

As Professor Hocking of Harvard observed years ago, there are more ways of getting lost today than ever before.

In worship — in quiet meditation and corporate prayer, in listening to God's word coming through the words read in Scripture lessons and in the words preached, in the hymns, in the sacraments of the presence and love of God, in the anthems and organ music offered as gifts of love to the Lover of beauty, truth, goodness, righteousness, and wholeness — we are found, and we find ourselves and are healed of our brokenness.

We are examined by Another whose compassion is greater than his wrath; and we examine ourselves. We do more; we bind

[4] Melvin E. Wheatley, sermon of September 18, 1966.

155

ourselves to the Highest, and in turn are bound by the Highest. There is a Power, a Truth, and a Love, made personal in Jesus Christ, that will never let us go.

"Going to church! You can't be serious!" And we say, without being on the defensive *"Oh, yes, we are, and we are serious about what is done there and what we may do there in our response to what God gives and asks.* We are going to church because we need to live our lives in the companionship of the best community there is." As Professor Gordon Allport wrote, "Religion to some of us is our audacious bid to bind ourselves to creation and to the Creator . . . to enlarge and complete our own personalities by finding the Supreme context in which we rightly belong." Let me put it simply: *Sometimes life is lonely for the most extroverted.* Others, including psychologist Harry Overstreet, have said that even when we are happy with our homes, our work, and our friends, we need a wider community with whom we can unashamedly care about the things we want to care about. In such a companionship, in such a community we can be open and easy, rather than solemnly rigid. Do we have such companionship in our churches? We are learning that every word we speak and every dollar we give to the church's total ministry can signal that we *care.*

God speaks to man in worship. Man speaks to God. Through the dialogue between God and man we learn both the demands and the promise of the living God. We then go out in mission. Thank God, the people of God get into every corner of the world. Often we falter, often we draw back, but then we come to worship God again, and keep our appointment with Christ. The remnant — the living church — becomes a mighty army with banners flying when it remembers that we are equally a worshiping and a witnessing community. Jesus "went to the synagogue, as his custom was, on the sabbath day." Can a disciple be greater than his Master and Lord? If you ever tried to let it all go — the church, the worship, the whole bit — did that really help?

PRAYER: O Lord Jesus whom not having seen except with the eyes of faith, we do love, though not enough. Give us thy grace, that in our worship of God we may learn who we are, where we are, where we want to be, and where we can find the power to go there; for thy love's sake. Amen.

156